Logo Life

Second printing, 2012
ISBN 978-90-6369-260-5

Text & design **Ron van der Vlugt**
Editing **Joy Maul-Phillips**
DTP **Alco Velders**

Published by **BIS Publishers**
'Het Sieraad', Postjesweg 1
1057 DT Amsterdam
The Netherlands
T (+) 31 (0)20 515 02 30
F (+) 31 (0)20 515 02 39
bis@bispublishers.nl
www.bispublishers.nl

Disclaimer
All brands, trademarks, names, images, logos and other intellectual property referenced in this book are the property of their respective owners. This independent publication is in no way affiliated with or authorized by, sponsored or otherwise endorsed by these owners, except where specifically requested by said owners. The intellectual property referenced in this book is merely used as an example of brands and logos in general.

While every effort has been made to trace all present copyright holders of the material in this book, any unintentional omission is hereby apologized for in advance, and we should of course be pleased to correct any errors in acknowledgements in any future editions of this book.

Ron van der Vlugt

LIFE HISTORIES OF 100 FAMOUS LOGOS

Logo Life

BIS Publishers

WINNER
BEST
MUSICAL
2009 TONY AWARD
BILLY
ELLIOT
THE MUSICAL
WHERE
MAXIMUM
PERFORMANCE
LIVES
maxell
www.maxell.com
MELROSE
PLACE
"THIS FEEL-GOOD MUSICAL
IS A PHENOMENON!"
MAMMA
MIA!
McDonald's
Restaurant
FRIDAYS

2009
TOSHIBA
TOSHIBA
TDK
3D DOUBLE FEATURE EVENT
ONLY IN THEATRES 2 WEEKS
TOY STORY
TOY STORY 2
RS
By Sheckler
THE LION KING
smile?
Helped injur
opponent wi
SPORTSMANSHI
Pass It O
Bankof merica

Previous pages:
Logo Life at Times Square, New York, USA, 2009 (Terabass)

LOGO LIFE

There's a good chance that you have already encountered the better part of the logos represented in this book today. Brands like Shell, Nike, Coca-Cola and McDonald's are omnipresent, and their logos are embedded in our collective memories. These logos seem to have been around for as long as we can remember. We grew up with them and they became part of our culture, our design context. These icons offer us comforting reassurance in this quickly changing visual world.

But where do these logos come from? What are their backgrounds, who designed them, and have they always looked like this? After all, why would they change in the first place? Why would companies invest so much energy and money in that transformation? Changing a major international brand is a multi-million dollar operation.

Despite the cost, logos do evolve. People change during the course of their lives, and so do companies, as well as their brands and logos. From humble beginnings, ambitions soar sky-high. In early years, companies might easily follow fashion styles to attain the image they desire, but they will settle down eventually. They engage in new relationships and want to look their best on the happiest day of their lives. The result is a burgeoning family of companies and brands. Some plead irreconcilable differences, separate and merge with a new partner. When mid-life crisis strikes, they simply get a facelift and dress to suit their new age – although it's not always an improvement. And then they grow old gracefully, turn 100 or more, and achieve a respectable old age, which is always a good opportunity to shine again. Companies, their brands and their logos will always be fine-tuning their appearance to stay relevant. They cannot afford not to, because there are always others waiting to take their positions in the spotlight.

The objective of the book before you was to collect an interesting mixture of logo histories of well-known international companies and brands to gain a better understanding of the reasons why logos look the way they do.
In most cases, there was a distinct point in time, very early on or much later in their logo lives, at which a decisive design solution was made that has defined all future designs. Can you imagine a future Renault logo without the diamond-shaped symbol?
Or Adidas not using the three stripes? When asked about the key to good design, Paul Rand described it in 1961 as "taking the essence of something that is already there and enhancing its meaning by putting it into a form everyone can identify with."

Logo Life shows the walk of life of 100 corporate and brand logos in alphabetical order. The logos covered here may not necessarily be the 100 best logos in the world, but surely many would be on such a list. Although many logo histories were obvious must-haves, Logo Life does not aspire to be a fully comprehensive reference work; a number of high-potential logos were not included due to space restrictions. Hopefully, your favorites have been included!

Ron van der Vlugt

CONTENTS

51 **KLM**
52 **Kmart**
53 **Kodak**
54 **Lego**
55 **Levi's**
56 **Lucky Strike**
57 **MasterCard**
58 **Mazda**
59 **McDonald's**
60 **Mercedes-Benz**
61 **Michelin**
62 **Microsoft**
63 **Mobil**
64 **MTV**
65 **NASA**
66 **Nickelodeon**
67 **Nike**
68 **Nikon**
69 **Nivea**
70 **Nokia**
71 **Opel**
72 **Pathé**
73 **Penguin**
74 **Pepsi**
75 **Pirelli**
76 **Qantas**
77 **Renault**
78 **Reuters**
79 **Rolex**
80 **Samsonite**
81 **Shell**
82 **Shiseido**
83 **Spar**
84 **Speedo**
85 **Starbucks**
86 **Target**
87 **Texaco**
88 **Total**
89 **Toyota**
90 **Toys "R" Us**
91 **Tupperware**
92 **UPS**
93 **Visa**
94 **Vodafone**
95 **Volkswagen**
96 **Volvo**
97 **Walmart**
98 **WWF**
99 **Xerox**
100 **The Y** (YMCA of the USA)

1 3M

1902, Two Harbors, MN, USA
Founders **Henry S. Bryan, Hermon W. Cable, John Dawn, William A. McGonagle, J. Danley Budd**
Company **3M Company** HQ **Maplewood, MN, USA**
www.3M.com

The earliest logo from the Minnesota Mining and Manufacturing Company is from a time when the company moved from Two Harbors to Duluth, Minnesota to focus on sandpaper products in the early 1900s.

Lacking corporate style guides during the first half of the 20th century, 3M would carry many different logos, some using the diamond in the middle with or without full company name and place of business. Note the difference in the 1938 logo as the company moved to Saint Paul. Others used only '3M' in many different typefaces.

From the 1950s on, oval shapes appeared, some wreathed in laurels to celebrate the company's 50th anniversary. These alternated with just typographic logos.

The highly inconsistent use of logos ended when Gerald Stahl Associates was asked to bring peace on the logo front and design a logo that unified the corporation and different business units. The result was a square industrial look. A corporate identity manual with a few approved versions of the logo was the result. Joseph C. Duke, 3M executive vice president, explained the logo's rationale in Advertising Age in 1961: "When one product, division or subsidiary makes a favorable impression anywhere, every other 3M division, subsidiary or product should benefit. In turn, the achievements and prestige of the 3M company should benefit each product and activity of the company."

In the 1970s, the company's focus changed from industrial abrasives and tapes to products for commercial and consumer markets. The 1978 'simple and smart' logo with the '3' and 'M' touching each other in Helvetica Black was designed by Siegel & Gale. Allen Siegel also pushed for a corporate color, vibrant red, and got his way. A timeless piece of design, it is still in use today and will probably remain so for many years to come.

3M's current sprayable permanent and repositionable adhesives

1906

1926

1926

1937

1938

1942

1944

3-M

1944

1948

1950

1951

1952

1954

1954

1955

1956

1960

3M

1960

1961, Gerald Stahl & Associates

1978, Siegel & Gale

2 7-ELEVEN

1927, Dallas, TX, USA
Founders **Joe C. Thompson Jr., John Jefferson Green** Company **7-Eleven, Inc.** HQ **Dallas, TX, USA**
www.7-eleven.com

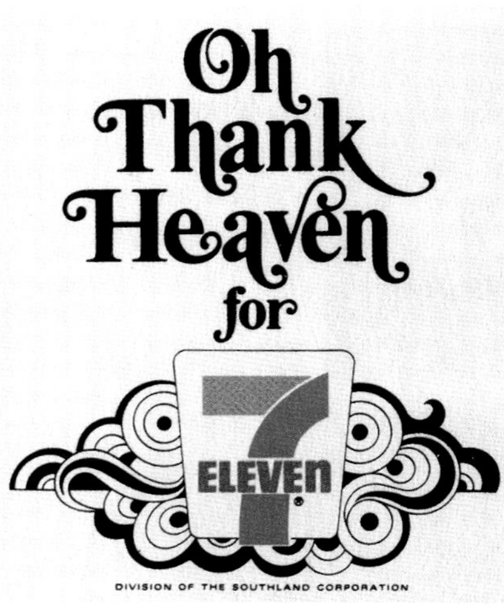

Left: 7-Eleven store, USA, 1960s (roadsidepictures). Right: 'Oh thank heaven for 7-Eleven', ad, 1970s

7-Eleven was founded as the Southland Ice Company in 1927. In that pre-refrigeration era, the company's 'ice houses' pioneered the convenience store concept. They sold large chunks of ice for home use, but also offered milk, bread and eggs. These stores stayed open when normal grocery stores were closed, increasing sales as well as customer satisfaction.

The first outlets were known as Tote'm stores, since customers 'toted' away their purchases. In 1946, an advertiser had the idea of naming the stores 7-Eleven to reflect the stores' new, extended hours - 7 a.m. until 11 p.m., seven days a week.

The first logo showed the word 'eleven' in capitals diagonally crossing a big seven in a green and red combination. The letter spacing in 'eleven' varied in the early logos and was much tighter on road signs, for example. In addition, the 'eleven' was not consistently placed at the same angle.

In the 1950s, the logo was restyled for better consistency, also improving readability by opening up the '7'. This more compact logo used a bold, condensed type for 'eleven' so the logo could be placed inside a tapered white shape and enclosed in a green circle.

The current 7-Eleven logo was introduced in 1969, featuring a two-toned '7' and rounded tapering shape, enclosed in a square. Note the use of a lowercase 'n' in the otherwise all-caps 'eleven' to maximize the boldness and readability of the condensed typeface. The storefront logo uses variable-width striping to brand the entire storefront.

1946

1950s

1969, Fran Gianninoto & Associates

Left: 'What a spot for a picnic', ad, 1960s
Below: Service and a friendly smile, 1966
Opposite: Storefront signing, 2010 (Simon Q)

WHAT A SPOT FOR A PICNIC

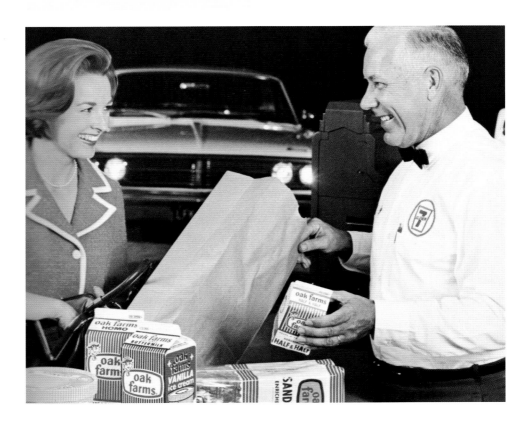

Just perfect! Right around the corner from the lake . . . A stone's throw from the mountains . . . A hoot and a holler from the beach . . . And just a couple of minutes from your own backyard. What a place for a picnic to start . . . with all the fixin's right there . . . right when you need them. Come on, let's go on a fun picnic. You bring the urge . . . We've got everything else.

OPEN 7 A.M. UNTIL 11 P.M.... 7 DAYS A WEEK

A DIVISION OF THE SOUTHLAND CORPORATION

ELEVEN

3 7UP

1920, St Louis, MO, USA
Founder **Charles Leiper Grigg** Company **Dr Pepper Snapple Group (USA), PepsiCo (outside USA)**
HQ **Plano, TX, USA** and **Purchase, NY, USA**
www.7up.com

Introduced as Bib-Label Lithiated Lemon-Lime Soda, Charles Leiper Grigg's company Howdy Corporation changed the name to 7UP when the bubbly drink grew more popular. It's still a bit of a mystery where the name came from, but early advertising featured a winged 7UP logo with copy that read: "A glorified drink in bottles only. Seven natural flavors blended into a savory, flavory drink with a real wallop."

In the 30s, the famous red square with the white logotype and bubbles appeared. The block lettering and underlining of 'UP' were inherited from the winged logo. Although it evolved slightly over the years, the logo survived over three decades, developing into iconic branding.

Around 1967, with the introduction of 'The Uncola' campaign, 7UP launched a simplified logo without bubbles, which used flat white typography in a rounded red square. The campaign set the brand apart from the competition and became part of a counter-culture that symbolized being true to yourself and challenging the status quo. From the 1980s, the 7UP logo included a red dot, representing the bubble, between the '7' and 'UP'. This dot has been animated and used as a cartoon mascot named Spot.

The 1990s mark the transition from red to green as the primary brand color for 7UP. It also gave the red spot the opportunity to become an important brand icon in its own right. It was also a time when the new vistas opened up by the computer made it possible to use all kinds of graphic effects, making the designs increasingly complicated in attempts to revitalize the brand.

In 2011, PepsiCo introduced a new logo for 7UP outside the USA which moved away from the drop shadows, 3D effects and graduated fills towards a cleaner aesthetic to reflect the new 'simpler is better' proposition. Three different styles are available on the various markets worldwide (graphic bubbles, graphic fruit and real fruit) to conform to local packaging rules.

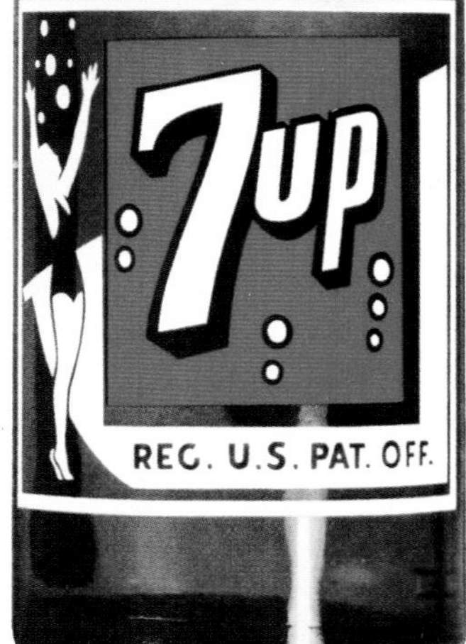

7UP bottle from the 1950s

1929

ca 1931

1940s

1950s

ca 1967

ca 1980

1990

1995

Right: 'Drink un anytime', decal sticker from the 'Uncola' campaign, ca 1967
Below: Packaging for twelve 355ml cans (outside USA), 2011

2000 *(USA)*

2007 *(outside USA)*

2007 *(outside USA)*

2010 *(USA)*

2011, TracyLocke *(outside USA)*

4 ADIDAS

1920, Herzogenaurach, Germany
Founder **Adi Dassler** Company **adidas AG**
HQ **Herzogenaurach, Germany**
www.adidas.com

Adi Dassler designed the three stripes himself, 1949
Note the first logo on the side of the left shoe (adidas AG)

The famous '3-Stripes' mark was created by founder Adi Dassler and first used on footwear in 1949. It represented comfort, durability and toughness, and made his footwear instantly recognizable when used in athletic competion. The brand logo consisted of a three-striped track & field shoe held up by the two 'd's as centrepiece of the logo.

Producing shoes for a wider variety of sports, adidas simplified its next-generation logo to just a logotype, with shortened 'd's. The logo became more compact in the 1960s, with even shorter 'd's lined up with a squared-off dot on the 'i' and tighter letter spacing. Offset by the circular 'a' and 'd' shapes, the result was the nicely balanced final stage of evolution for the logotype.

When adidas expanded into the apparel sector in the late 60s, it needed a new brand logo. Inspired by the 3-Stripes, the 1971 'Trefoil' logo (chosen from more than 100 proposals) was introduced in the 1972 Summer Olympics in Munich. The three leaves and their triple intersection symbolize the Olympic spirit, as well as the diversity of the brand.

The 1990 '3 bars' logo was developed for the equipment range of performance products. It is inspired by the three stripes as they appear on footwear. The sloping bars represent a mountain, indicating the challenges to be faced.

In 2002, with the merger of adidas and Salomon, a new structure was developed comprising three divisions: Sport Heritage (Trefoil logo), Sport Performance (3 bars logo) and Sport Style (the logo showing the three stripes speeding around the globe, representing the future and the fast-moving ever-changing world).

In 2005, after the divestiture of Salomon, a new brand logo was introduced as a catch-all for the logos of the three divisions.

World Cup match ball 'Team spirit', 2006 (adidas AG)

1949

1950s

1960s

1971

1990, Peter Moore

2002

2005

adidas
adidas

adidas adiPure, 2011
Opposite top: Soccer fans cheering for the German national team (adidas AG)
Opposite below: Soccer player David Beckham and basketball player Kevin Garnett were two of the celebrities to take part in Adidas' Originals House Party film, celebrating '60 Years of Soles and Stripes'. The advert was released in cinemas and on TV, 2009 (adidas AG)

5 AEG

1887, Berlin, Germany
Founder **Emil Rathenau** Parent Company **AB Electrolux** HQ **Stockholm, Sweden**
www.aeg.com

The first logo for the German electrical equipment producer *Allgemeine Elektrizitäts Gesellschaft* (General Electricity Company), or AEG, was actually designed as a sign for the employee entrance gate of the offices.

The big change came in 1907 when AEG hired architect Peter Behrens as an artistic consultant. Behrens invented the concept of the corporate identity by standardizing the branding and look of graphic design, advertising, product design and architecture.

This period of mass production made industrial consumer goods affordable for increasing numbers of people. In line with the constantly changing nature of the business, the logo changed several times in a very short period. When the hexagon shaped logo was finally replaced by the boxed-in, all-caps AEG, the logo with the characteristic serifs stayed virtually unchanged until the present day.

Electrolux, owner of the AEG brand since 2004, started to double-brand the household appliances in 2005. This logo was simplified in 2011, putting the Electrolux symbol in front of the AEG logotype. Although the double branding continues for that product range, the logo continues to be used for all other product groups, including consumer electronics and telecom.

Top right: Poster, ca 1908
Right: AEG Favola Plus LM5250, 2011

1887, Franz Schwechten

ca 1900, Otto Eckermann

1907, Peter Behrens

1907, Peter Behrens

1908, Peter Behrens

1908, Peter Behrens

1960

2000

2005 *(household appliances only)*

2011 *(household appliances only)*

6 AIR FRANCE

1933, Paris, France
Founders **Air Orient, Air Union, Compagnie Générale Aéropostale, Compagnie Internationale de Navigation Aérienne (CIDNA), Société Générale de Transport Aérienne (SGTA)**
Company **Air France S.A.** HQ **Paris-Charles de Gaulle Airport, France**
www.airfrance.com

Above: Original Air Orient logo with hippocampe *symbol, ca 1929.*
Right: The legendary Concorde, 1977

The winged seahorse (called *hippocampe ailé* or *la crevette*) used by Air Orient, one of the founding companies, was incorporated into the Air France logo at the airline's inception in 1933.

Air France became the flag carrier after nationalization of all French airlines in 1945. Logos were not used consistently then and many variations were seen, like the 1949 logo with the *hippocampe* inside the letter 'C'.

With the arrival of the commercial jetliners around 1960, Air France redesigned its identity. Roger Excoffon's Antique Olive Bold formed the basis of the new logo. The *hippocampe* still played its role as a mark of quality, but was not part of the logo.

The speed stripes, referencing the national flag, were introduced in 1975, integrated into the wing of the *hippocampe*. The Antique Olive Bold remained the logotype, as would be the case in the 1990 restyling.

After privatization in 1999 and the 2000 creation of SkyTeam, a global alliance of a group of international airlines, Air France merged with KLM in 2004. Now one of the largest air transport groups in the world, Air France KLM continued to use Air France and KLM as separate brands.

The 2009 redesign produced a cleaner, sleeker look, expressing the core values of Excellence, the Art of Travelling, and the Human Touch. The collection of speed stripes and the Olive Bold font, which survived three logos and more than four decades, gave way to a sophisticated logotype and a single dynamic stripe. The two words of the company's name were combined into a single word in the logo, but remain separate in written copy.

As part of the new brand identity, the *hippocampe* was transformed into a beautifully crafted wireframe. Also, for the first time, Air France integrated an AF monogram into its identity program.

1933

AIR FRANCE

1949

AIR FRANCE

1961, Roger Excoffon and José Mendoza

1975

1990

2009, Brand Image

7 AKZO NOBEL

1792, Groningen, Netherlands
Founder **Wiert Willem Sikkens** Company **Akzo Nobel NV** HQ **Amsterdam, Netherlands**
www.akzonobel.com

One of the largest chemical companies in the world, AkzoNobel has a product portfolio covering decorative paints, performance coatings and specialty chemicals. Its history can be traced back to 1792, when Wiert Willem Sikkens founded Sikkens Lacquers. The Sikkens brand is still part of AkzoNobel.

AkzoNobel has a very long history of mergers and divestments, but one of the most significant in its history is the merger between the Algemeene Kunstzijde Unie (AKU) and Koninklijke Zout Organon (KZO), forming Akzo in 1969. A folded bold line, forming a triangular letter A, became the first symbol for Akzo, placed above the name.

The 350 companies that fell under Akzo had continued to build their own brands without emphasizing their relationship with Akzo. Despite major expansion up to the mid-1980s, the company was almost entirely invisible to the public eye. According to one description, it was the biggest 'unknown company' in the world. Unwilling to stay permanently in the background, Akzo resolved to fulfill its true potential.

The all-embracing figure was inspired by a Greek sculpture from 450 BC. Representing the human factor in the equation, it symbolized Akzo's entrepreneurial culture. By consistently using the logo throughout the corporation, Akzo unified the visual branding for its diverse subsidiaries.

Six years later, in 1994, Akzo merged with Nobel Industries to form AkzoNobel. Nobel Industries' roots go back to 1646 and also to the famous Swedish chemist Alfred Nobel. The figure, nicknamed 'Bruce' since 2001 after the young son of an AkzoNobel Chicago office employee, remained untouched.

In 2007, AkzoNobel acquired ICI. To express the innovative character of the company, AkzoNobel updated its identity in 2008, losing the space between the words and adding an all-new 'Bruce' who seems to be looking at the sun and reaching for the future. The brand book states: "A united and determined AkzoNobel has the right symbol for the coming decades, a symbol with forcefulness and humanity—and continuity, too."

Left: 'Delivering tomorrow's answers today', annual report 2009. Right: AkzoNobel HQ, Amsterdam, 2011 (Akzo Nobel NV)

1969

1988, Wolff Olins

1994

2008, Saffron

8 ALFA ROMEO

1910, Milan, Italy
Founders **Alexandre Darracq, Ugo Stella, Nicola Romeo**
Company **Fiat Group Automobiles S.p.A.** HQ **Turin, Italy**
www.alfaromeo.com

Left: Coat of arms of the Visconti family
Right: Coat of arms of the City of Milan

The Alfa Romeo logo, which is incorporated into a portfolio of car badges, consists of two symbols that reference the city of Milan, where the cars were manufactured. The red cross represents Milan, while the serpent devouring the enemy is the coat of arms of the Visconti family. The idea to use the serpent came from a young designer from the technical department who saw the serpent on the Filarete tower while he was waiting for a tram in Piazza Castello.

The red cross and the serpent were enclosed by a blue circle with the words 'ALFA' ('Anonima Lombarda Fabbrica Automobili') and 'MILANO', separated by two knots symbolizing the House of Savoy that ruled Italy at the time. Some time later, the fragile serif lettering was changed to a bold sans serif for better readability.

When Nicola Romeo bought the Alfa factory in 1915, he added his name to the brand. After Alfa Romeo achieved a legendary victory in the first World Driving Championship with the 'P2' in 1924, a crown of laurels was added to the logo in 1925.

Following the fall of the monarchy and the proclamation of the Italian Republic, the knots were replaced by two wavy lines. Right after the war, a sober-colored badge seemed the appropriate thing to place on the cars.

From around 1950, the multi-colored logo was installed again. When part of Alfa Romeo's production was moved to the south of Italy in 1972, 'Milano' was dropped from the logo and the hyphen between the words was removed, causing ALFAROMEO to be read as one word.

The logo still in use today was unveiled in 1982, reintroducing a space between the words and using gold lettering. This version actually represents a 3D car badge.

Newspaper ad for Alfa Romeo 1600 GT Veloce, 1960s

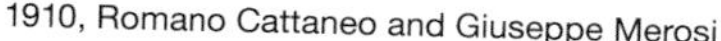
1910, Romano Cattaneo and Giuseppe Merosi

ca 1912

1915

1925

1945

1950

1972

1982

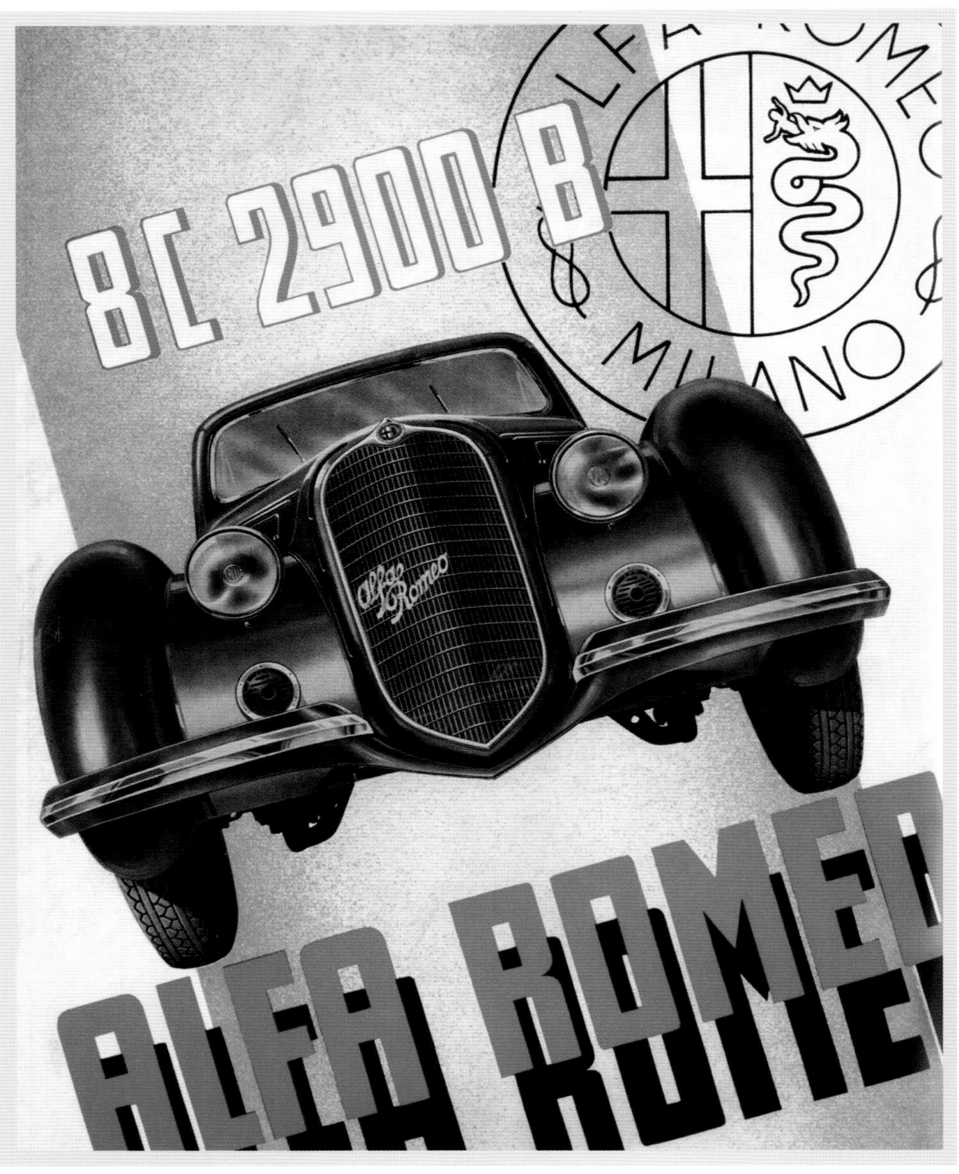

Alfa Romeo 8C 2900B, poster, ca 1937
Opposite: Alfa Romeo Giulietta front grill, 1950s

ALFA-ROMEO
MILANO

9 ALLIANZ

1890, Berlin and Munich, Germany
Founders **Carl Thieme, Wilhelm Finck** Company **Allianz SE** HQ **Munich, Germany**
www.allianz.com

When it was founded in Munich in 1890, with its base of operations in Berlin, financial services firm Allianz designed a logo that showed the imperial eagle (the German national symbol) holding the coats of arms of both cities: a monk (Munich) and a bear (Berlin). By 1918, Allianz had become Germany's largest insurer.

When the company name changed to Allianz Group in 1923, the logo was redesigned. The stylized eagle by Karl Schulpig was depicted holding three young egrets, symbolizing the new subsidiaries.

Building on its international presence from the early 1970s, Allianz introduced a modernized logo in 1977. Hansjörg Dorschel designed the logo using an uppercase and lowercase brand name. The more abstract eagle and its young were enclosed in a circle, expressing the company's global aspirations.

In response to the globalizing financial markets and the company's expanding financial services, the logo was further restyled in 1999, following a wave of international mergers. The new logo was much friendlier than its somewhat aggressive-looking predecessor. Stripped down to three vertical strokes, the eagle no longer carried its young. Instead, it cleverly used the letter 'I' of the new logotype as its body, with the serif symbolizing the head.

The Allianz Arena, Munich, Germany (Richard Bartz)

1899

ALLIANZ

1923, Karl Schulpig

1977, Hansjörg Dorschel

1999, Claus Koch

10 AMERICAN AIRLINES

1930, New York, NY, USA
Founders **82 independent airlines**
Parent Company **AMR Corporation** HQ **Fort Worth, TX, USA**
www.aa.com

American Airlines ticket envelope, USA, 1930s

American Airways, an umbrella brand for a collection of independent carriers, was founded in 1930. The searchlight beacon was its first logo, inspired by the lighted air routes that marked the flight path between Texas and California.

The landing eagle dividing the two 'A's was introduced in 1932, when the company was still called American Airways. In 1934, American Airways was renamed American Airlines after E.L. Cord bought the company. The brand name was occasionally integrated into the badge along with the services 'Mail', 'Passengers' and 'Express'. A flash in the background and detailing on the eagle were added.

After WWII, the logo was restyled. The eagle, now flying from left to right, was placed on a white background. A separate brand name was added in different ways.

The jet era called for a redesign, which resulted in a simplified eagle and an oval enclosure in the early 60s. The full brand name, or the shorter 'American', was added both inside and outside the oval.

Italian designer Massimo Vignelli designed the famous 1967 logo, with the significantly simplified eagle landing in the white space created by the mountainous double Helvetica 'A' in the American national colors of red, white and blue.

The logo has been restyled twice since then. At first, the eagle was stripped down to the essentials: the feathers melted into solid wings and the head and talons were streamlined. This pared-down version appears to have been less popular, since the feathered edges on the eagle's wings and tail were reintroduced.

American Airlines 757-200, 2011

1930

1932

1934

ca 1946

ca 1963

1967, Massimo Vignelli

1980s

1990s

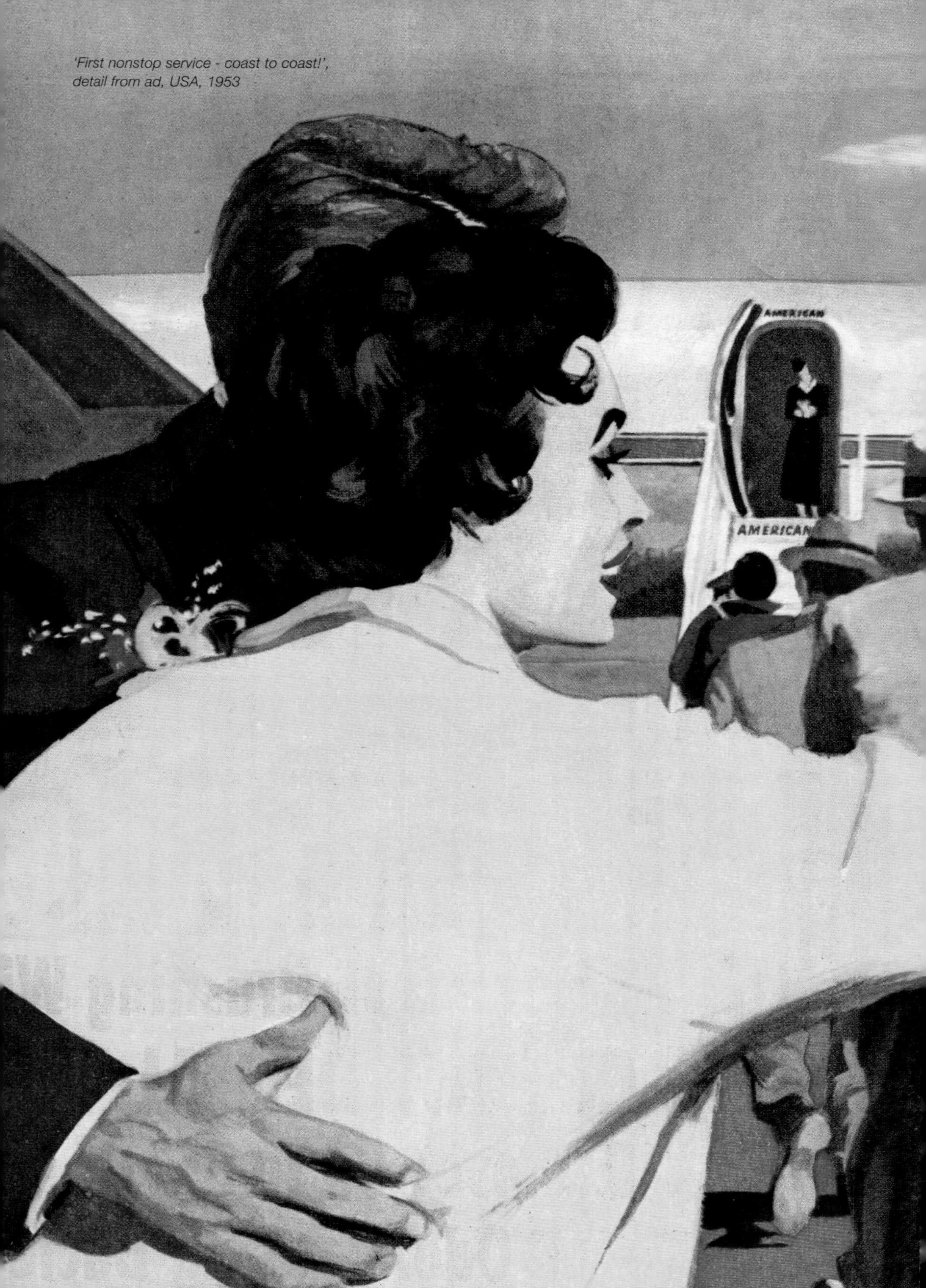

'First nonstop service - coast to coast!',
detail from ad, USA, 1953

D 7 C
N303AA
AMERICAN
AA

11 APPLE

1976, Cupertino, CA, USA
Founders **Steve Jobs, Steve Wozniak, Ronald Wayne** Company **Apple Inc.** HQ **Cupertino, CA, USA**
www.apple.com

Introduction campaign for the Apple iPad, New York, USA, 2010

Apple's first logo was a complex picture, a tribute to Isaac Newton sitting under an apple tree, with a phrase from Wordsworth: 'Newton...a mind forever voyaging through strange seas of thought...alone', along with the name Apple Computer Co.

Hard to reproduce, it was soon replaced by Rob Janoff's 'Rainbow Apple' logo, with the introduction of the Apple II in 1977. In a later interview, Rob Janoff said that there was no real brief. Steve Jobs only told him not to make it "too cute". Ironically, the logo was designed by hand, using pencil and strips of paper.

The colors represented the monitor's ability to reproduce colors, a unique selling point at the time. Its bright colors were intended to be appealing to young people.

The bite was added so that people would still recognize it as an apple rather than a cherry. According to Janoff, it does not represent the computing term 'byte', nor is there any biblical reference. Also, the bite fit snugly around the first letter of the brand name in Motter Tektura, a typeface that was considered cutting-edge at the time.

In 1984, with the introduction of the Apple Macintosh, the less than mathematically precise curves of the original logo were refined. The brand name was dropped at that point, since the apple alone proved to be an iconic symbol for the company.

From 1998 on, with the roll-out of the colorful iMacs, the stylish monochromatic themes of the logo were used, which perfectly matched the innovative character of the products.

1976, Ronald Wayne

1977, Rob Janoff

1984, Landor Associates

1998, Apple

1998-2007, Apple

Top: Colorful iMacs, 1998
Far left: Apple I operation manual, 1976
Left: 'A is for Apple', ad, USA, 1977
Opposite: Apple Store illuminated sign, Shanghai, China, 2010 (Simon Q)

Everlasting

12 AT&T

1877, Boston, MA, USA
Founder **Gardiner Greene Hubbard** Company **AT&T Inc** HQ **Dallas, TX, USA**
www.att.com

The Bell Telephone Company, named after Alexander Graham Bell, credited with inventing the first working telephone, was founded in 1877 by Gardiner Green Hubbard. After several mergers, it became the American Telephone & Telegraph Company in 1885.

The Bell system was the telephone service covering the USA from 1877 to 1984, provided by all AT&T-owned telephone companies. These subsidiaries were known as Bell Operating Companies (BOCs).

From 1921, this concept was visualized in the logo. The subsidiary could put its own name in the outer ring along with AT&T as the parent company. The Bell System icon in the center was the same for all the 22 BOCs.

A classic evolution of increasingly simplified bell icons continued until 1984, when a federal mandate forced AT&T to break up in separate companies as a result of antitrust laws, and the Bell System effectively ceased to exist. Stripped back to the very core, the highlight at the end of this road was unquestionably Saul Bass' 1969 version.

After the Bell System was dismantled, Saul Bass designed a layered globe with a 3D effect to replace the bell. It was restyled again in 2000 in an attempt to bring the logo into the 21st century.

In 2005, the AT&T Corporation was purchased by SBC Communication, formerly known as Southwestern Bell Corporation. Once a regional BOC, it had been founded in 1983 when the Bell System was dismantled. After the merger, the AT&T Inc. logo was a restyled, semi-transparent globe with the brand name in lowercase letters.

Left: 'American Telephone and Telegraph company', early brochure, USA, 1899. Right: AT&T service vans, 2011

1889

1900

1921

1939

1964

1969, Saul Bass

1983, Saul Bass

2000

2005, Interbrand

IT'S FUN TO 'PHONE!

Turn a few minutes into fun by calling a friend or loved one. Whether it's down the street, or across the country, a sunny get-together makes the day a lot brighter. Lonely feelings are laughed away by a cheerful visit by telephone. So treat yourself to a welcome break and just for fun—call someone!

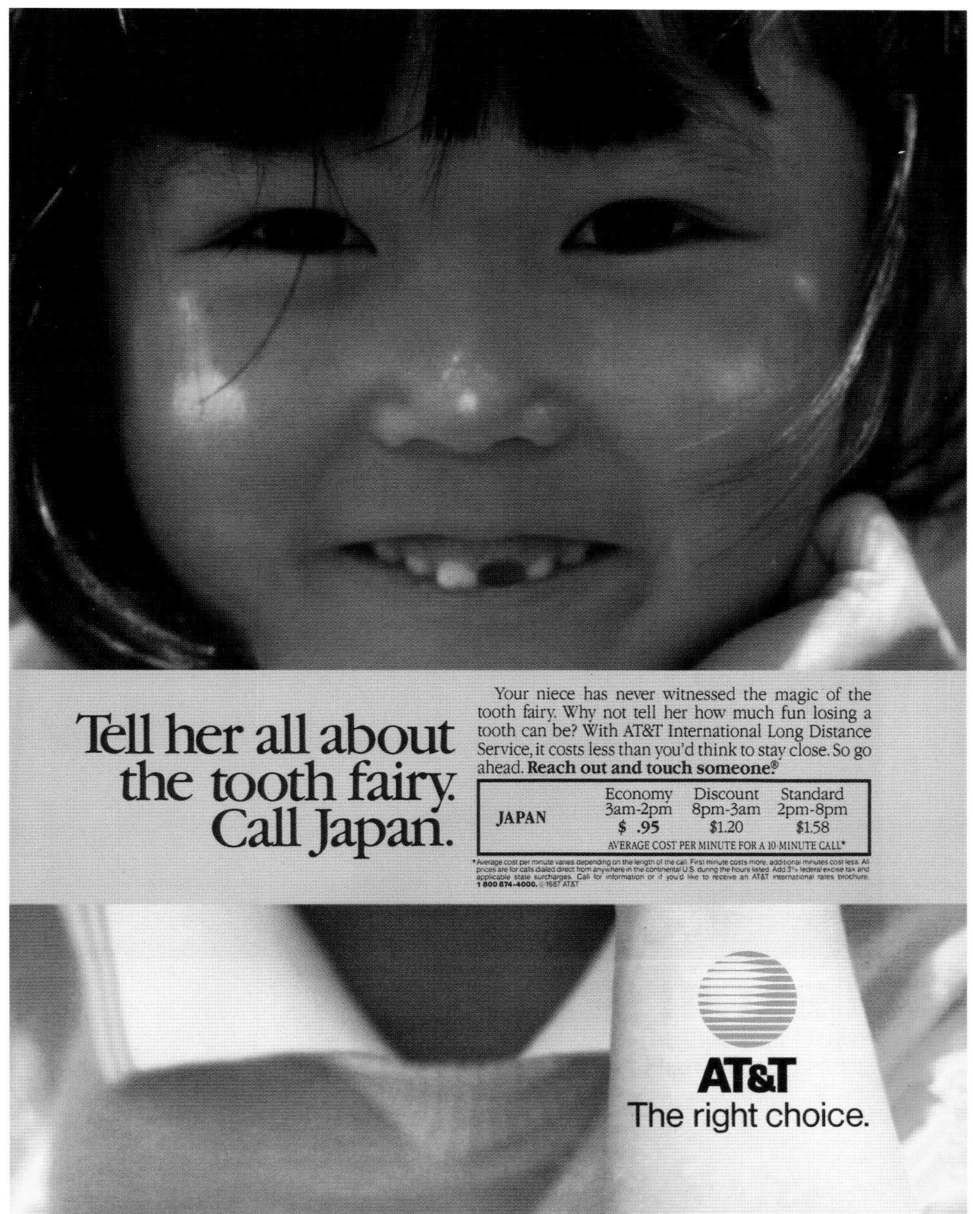

Tell her all about the tooth fairy. Call Japan.
Your niece has never witnessed the magic of the tooth fairy. Why not tell her how much fun losing a tooth can be? With AT&T International Long Distance Service, it costs less than you'd think to stay close. So go ahead. Reach out and touch someone.®
JAPAN
Economy 3am-2pm $ .95
Discount 8pm-3am $1.20
Standard 2pm-8pm $1.58
AVERAGE COST PER MINUTE FOR A 10-MINUTE CALL*
*Average cost per minute varies depending on the length of the call. First minute costs more, additional minutes cost less. All prices are for calls dialed direct from anywhere in the continental U.S. during the hours listed. Add 3% federal excise tax and applicable state surcharges. Call for information or if you'd like to receive an AT&T international rates brochure. 1 800 874-4000. © 1987 AT&T
AT&T
The right choice.

'Tell her all about the tooth fairy', ad, USA, 1988
Opposite: 'It's fun to 'phone!', ad starring Betsy Bell, USA, 1958

13 AUDI

1909, Zwickau, Germany
Founder **August Horch**
Company **Audi AG** HQ **Ingolstadt, Germany**
www.audi.com

The first Audi logo was designed in Art Nouveau style. The logotype with flower-inspired motifs was enclosed by an oval.

It was Lucian Bernhard, one of Germany's leading typeface designers, who created a new, modern Audi logotype in 1919. It would characterize the brand until 2009.

In 1922, Audi announced a competition for a new car emblem to complement the logotype. 150 entries were submitted; the chosen logotype was the '1' on top of a globe designed by Prof. Arno Dresschers. Registered in 1923, it appeared on the radiator grills of all Audis until production ceased in 1940.

The depression forced Audi, DKW, Horch and Wanderer to join forces in 1932 to cut costs, above all by standardizing chassis frames. The new company, Auto Union AG, would serve as an umbrella brand for the four car brands. The famous rings were born, symbolizing the endless unity of the companies.

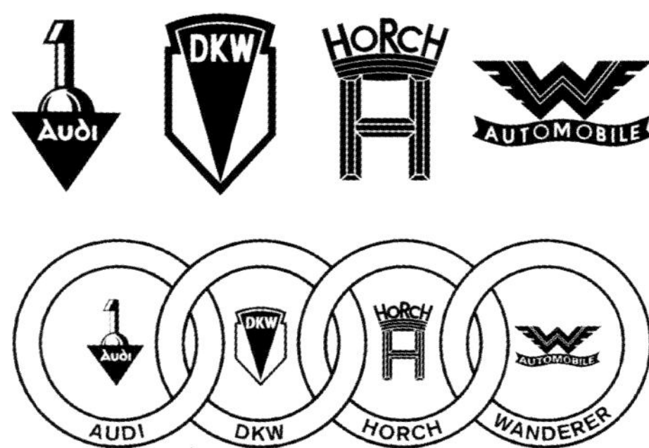

Four separate logos were combined in 1932 with the formation of Auto Union AG

Audi urban concept Spyder, 2011 (Audi AG)

The four companies used their individual logos in combination with the Auto Union logo. However, the unified Auto Union logo was used for all motor sports activities from 1933 on.

After WWII, the company moved to Ingolstadt and the new company, Auto Union GmbH, started the production of DKW vans, cars and motorcycles, bearing the four rings. However, when the Volkswagen Group acquired the company in 1965, the new models were produced under the Audi brand.

Although the rings were removed from the logo in 1978, which resulted in a version very similar to the 1919 logo, they remained on the front grill.

In 1994, the four rings were reinstated as the company's principal image. As part of Audi's centennial celebration in 2009, the logo was given restyled metal rings and a new logotype that broke free of Bernhard's style.

1909

1919, Lucian Bernhard

1923, Prof. Arno Dresscher

1932

1965

1978

1994, Meta Design

2009, Meta Design

Audi
Audiwerke A. G.
Zwickau-Sa.

Replica of a 1937 Auto Union Type C
16-cylinder Streamliner, 2009 (Audi AG)
Opposite: Audi poster, Germany, ca 1925

14 BARBIE

1959, CA, USA
Creator **Ruth Handler** Company **Mattel, Inc.** HQ **El Segundo, CA, USA**
www.barbie.com www.mattel.com

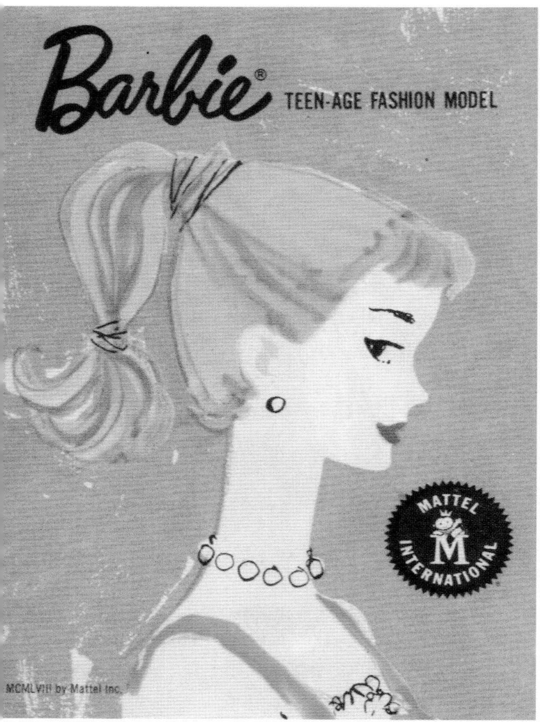

'Barbie, teen-age fashion model', brochure cover, USA, 1958

Founded in 1945, Mattel would be known for the most famous and successful doll ever created. Ruth Handler, her husband Elliot, and their close friend Harold Mattson formed the company, deriving the name from 'Matt' for Mattson and 'el' for Elliot.

It was Ruth Handler who envisioned the Barbie doll, named after her daughter Barbara. Barbie was introduced at the New York Toy Show in March 1959, after a patent had been obtained in the previous year.

Two years later, in 1961, Barbie's boyfriend Ken would be named after Ruth and Elliot's son Ken. Barbie's first logo was a cheerful, jumping script with a pig-tailed capital 'B'. In the fashion of the time, a heavy drop shadow was added around 1970.

To keep the logo up-to-date, a completely new logo appeared in 1977, building on the curly B of the previous logos, again with a heavy drop shadow. The 1980s restyling of the shadow effect was followed in 1992 by a new, more sophisticated logotype that used subtle curls.

Returning to its more playful roots, the logo was redesigned again in 2000, based more closely on its original form. Two other scripts followed soon after, the first with a flower dot on the 'i'. Eventually, when Barbie celebrated her 50th anniversary in 2009, the first Barbie logo was reinstalled in the signature pink (PMS 291) and accompanied by a roundel depicting Barbie's ponytailed silhouette.

50th anniversary Barbie and logo, 2009

1959

1970

1977

1984

1992

2000

2003

2005

2009

15 **BASF**

1865, Mannheim, Germany
Founder **Friedrich Engelhorn** Company **BASF SE** HQ **Ludwigshafen, Germany**
www.basf.com

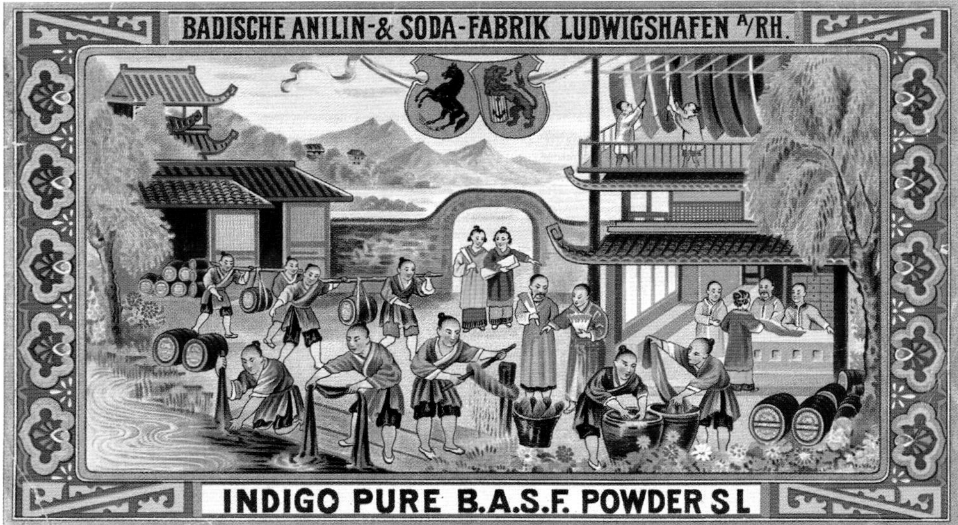

Indigo powder packaging label, ca 1903 (© BASF SE)

In 1865, when Badische Anilin- und Soda-fabrik started its business activities, there seemed to be no need for a logo. BASF's first logo was introduced in 1873. It combined two elements: the horse which originates from the coat of arms of the city of Stuttgart, and the official seal of Ludwigshafen/Rhine. The seal depicts the Bavarian lion holding a signboard bearing an anchor. The logo visualized the merger of BASF with the companies Knosp and Siegle, both located in Stuttgart.

Registered as a trademark in 1922, the 'BASF egg' was initially only used by the fertilizers division. For the export markets, the 'Horse and Lion' logo was replaced by a logo which was easy to understand in many countries and cultures. It combined the egg as a universal symbol of life and growth with the acronym of the company name. This logo was used unchanged until the end of WWII.

From 1955, the two parts were further divided into four, one for each initial. An alternative version had a garland of corn wrapped around the lower part of the logo.

BASF's traditional 'Horse and Lion' logo was redesigned in 1952. The BASF lettering embedded in a crown was added, as well as the founding year date 1865, all enclosed in a circular frame. This design remained in use until the end of the 1960s.

1873/75

1922

1952

BASF BASF

1953

1955

1968

1985

The Chemical Company

2004, Jörg Zintzmeyer

One year later, in 1953, a logotype was introduced that used robust condensed lettering (in both outline and solid versions). It was used simultaneously with the 'Horse and Lion' logo, starting with the announcement of the company's re-establishment after the war.

Soon referred to as the 'briquet', the black rectangle with the white sans serif BASF lettering marked a new era of the corporate design starting in 1968. The corporate typeface specifications, however, included both Helvetica and Englische Schreibschrift.

In 1973, the company name Badische Anilin- & Soda-Fabrik AG was changed to BASF Aktiengesellschaft. As part of that shift, the four letters 'BASF' changed from an acronym to a proper name. In the late 1960s, the desire for a more modern corporate design system became more obvious, and in 1986 the free-standing bold BASF letters became the new logo. Electronic typesetting systems offered new technical possibilities to realize delicate changes in shapes and kerning. At this point, the logo artwork was derived from the characters of a New Helvetica font. This logo was used throughout the BASF group until 2004.

Starting in March 2004, the visual identity of the BASF brand was relaunched in a new corporate design. The familiar BASF lettering was combined with a square component, symbolizing partnership, cooperation, and mutual success for BASF and its business partners. BASF now calls itself 'The Chemical Company', as an expression of its leading position in the chemical industry.

Six corporate colors support the perception of flexibility and diversity, and a layout system governs the consistent appearance of the BASF brand across all media.

The 'briquet' logo and its successor were not only used as the corporate brand logo, but also to combine the BASF brand with the symbols of two major product ranges. Printing systems used the yellow signet (ca.1968-2002). The first version of the spiral logo of the magnetic tapes business dates back to 1950. By 1954, the red color was part of the design. The combination of the red spiral with the BASF lettering became a well-known symbol for the audio and video tape cassettes which BASF manufactured until 1996.

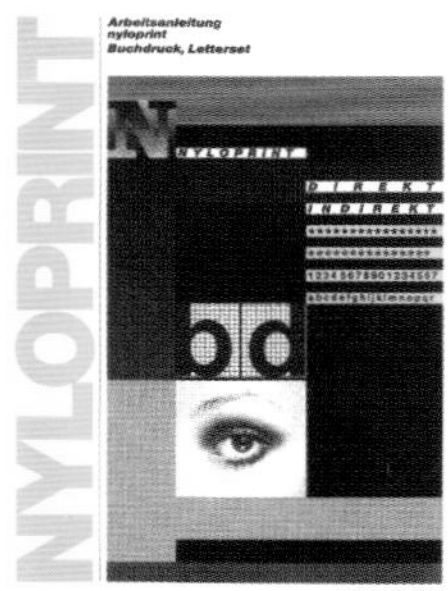

Left: Nyloprint manual, Germany, 1982 (© BASF SE)
Right: 'BASF compact cassettes. Precision made in Germany', ad, Germany, 1981 (© BASF SE)

Opposite: 'Kids love chemistry', corporate ad, 2011 (© BASF SE) (one of the themes used in the corporate advertising campaign that was launched that year)

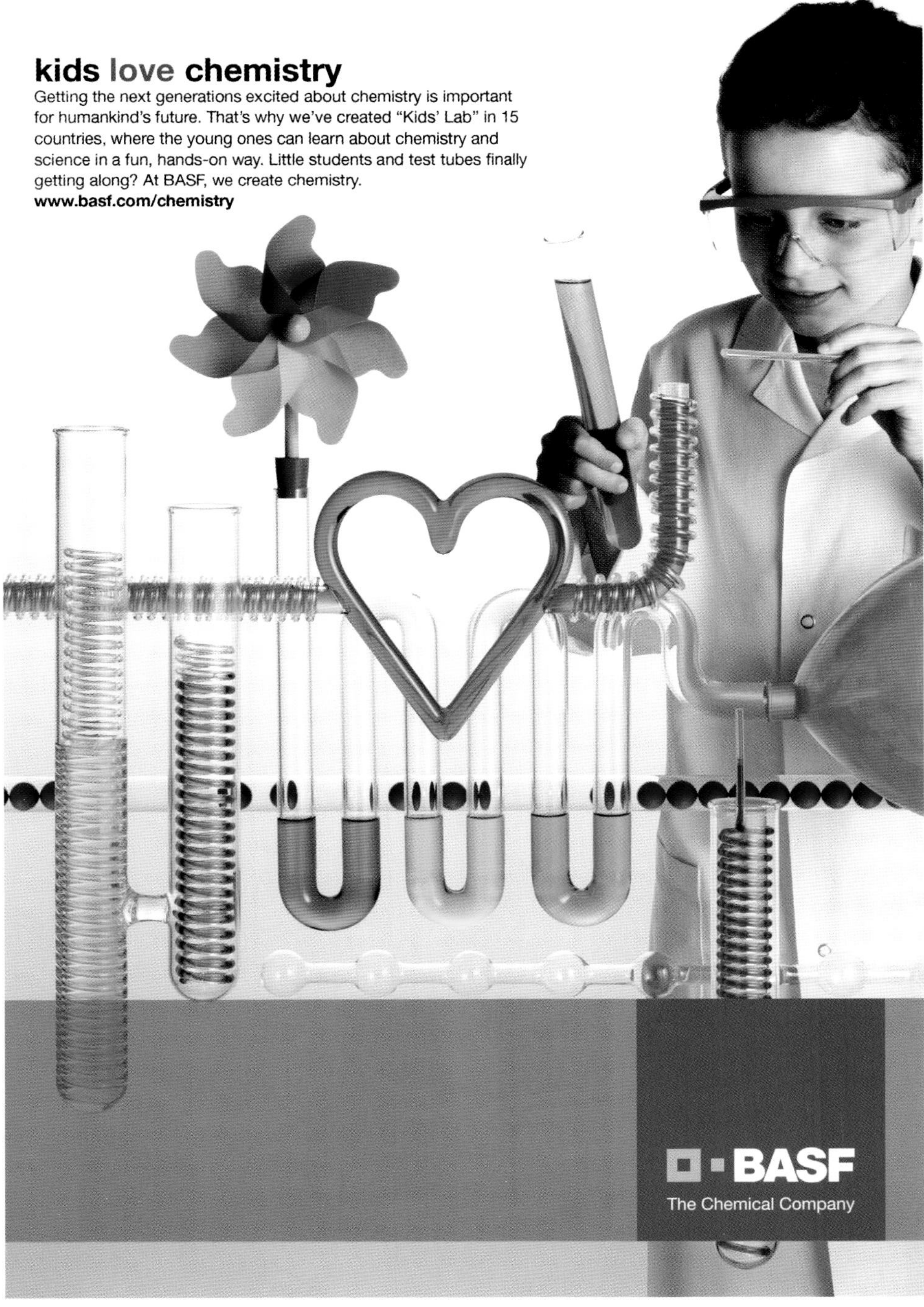
kids love chemistry
Getting the next generations excited about chemistry is important for humankind's future. That's why we've created "Kids' Lab" in 15 countries, where the young ones can learn about chemistry and science in a fun, hands-on way. Little students and test tubes finally getting along? At BASF, we create chemistry.
www.basf.com/chemistry
BASF
The Chemical Company

16 BASKIN ROBBINS

1945, Glendale, USA
Founders **Burt Baskin, Irv Robbins** Parent Company **Dunkin' Brands** HQ **Glendale, CA, USA**
www.baskin-robbins.com

Burt's Ice Cream Shop and Snobird Ice Cream, owned by brothers-in-law Burt Baskin and Irv Robbins, started at the advice of Irv's father. It wasn't until 1953 that the ice cream chain dropped the separate identities and became Baskin Robbins. They soon became very well known for their '31 flavors' slogan - although when the very first Baskin Robbins store opened, it only offered 21 flavors.

The 31 flavors concept, one for every day of the month, came from Carson Roberts advertising agency (which later became Ogilvy & Mather). '31' therefore became an important element of the logo. Carson Roberts also advised the pink (cherry) and brown (chocolate) polka dots and Western-style typeface that referred to clowns, circuses, carnivals and fun.

A much more serious logo was introduced in 1988, with blue replacing the brown. The semi-circle outlined a scoop of ice cream on top of a cone.

In 2005, a new brand identity was established as part of the company's 60th anniversary celebration. The logo was intended to capture the fun and energy of Baskin Robbins. Offering a wide range of ice creams, drinks, and cakes, the focus was shifted to the brand name itself. Without losing its roots, '31' was cleverly hidden away in the 'BR' initials of the sharp-edged dancing font.

Baskin Robbins ice cream parlor, USA, 1950s (Dunkin' Brands)
Right: Two-scoop waffle cone, 2011

1953

1988, Lippincott & Margulies

2005

17 BAYER

1863, Barmen (now part of Wuppertal)**, Germany**
Founders **Friedrich Bayer, Johann Friedrich Weskott**
Company **Bayer AG** HQ **Leverkusen, Germany**
www.bayer.com

The chemical and pharmaceutical company Bayer was founded in 1863 as 'Friedrich Bayer et comp.' by dye salesman Friedrich Bayer and master dyer Johann Friedrich Weskott, manufacturing synthetic dyestuffs.

Bayer was transformed into a joint stock company in 1881, called Farbenfabriken vorm. Friedr. Bayer & Co. The first Bayer logo depicted a lion with the grid on which Saint Lawrence was martyred. It was based on the coat of arms of the city of Elberfeld, where Bayer was headquartered at the time. The level of detail makes it hard to see, but a helmet and a series of other decorations were added in 1886.

Bayer developed into a chemical company operating internationally. The logo was redesigned in 1895. It showed a winged lion holding a caduceus standing against the globe, to illustrate self-confidence and openness to the world. Bayer's biggest success came with the invention of the 'drug of the century', Aspirin, which was launched onto the market in 1899.

'Genuine Bayer Aspirin', detail from ad, USA, 1920s

Bayer sign gets cleaned at Cologne-Bonn Airport, Germany, 2006 (Bayer AG)

Increasing export was one of the reasons for the new, simpler logo of 1904, called 'the Bayer Cross', which was designed by Bayer employee Hans Schneider. The word 'Bayer' was written horizontally and vertically, intersecting at the 'Y'. Bayer's Aspirin was exclusively available from pharmacists and doctors. Since that precluded the option of branded packaging, the Bayer Cross was imprinted on the tablets for recognition.

In 1929, the Cross was modernized and adopted the look of the actual Aspirin tablet; it has hardly changed since. The Bayer Cross became the most important element of the company's image and acts as a seal of quality for Bayer's products and services worldwide. A Bayer logotype and two green and blue bars were added in 1989.

In 2002, Bayer became a management holding company with legally independent operating subgroups (HealthCare, Chemicals, and CropScience) acting under the common Bayer umbrella. The Bayer Cross became three-dimensional and incorporated the company's colors to give the logo a modern and relevant design without impairing its recognizability. As part of a clarifying branding structure, the Cross was slightly changed in 2010, removing the 3D effects for a stronger logo.

1881

1886

1895

1904, Hans Schneider

(logo used for export)

1929

1989

2002 *(added logotype is used only in exceptional circumstances)*

2010

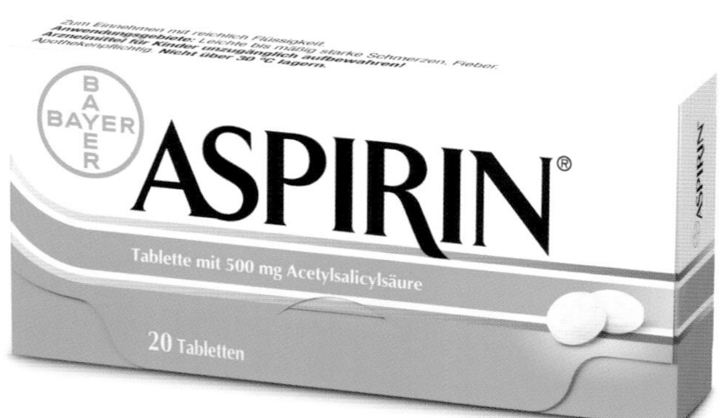

Top: Huge illuminated sign (51 meters in diameter and lit by 1710 bulbs) overlooks Bayer's hometown of Leverkusen, Germany, 2006 (Bayer AG)
Above: Aspirin packaging, Germany, 2011
Opposite: 250-gram bottle of Aspirin powder, Germany, 1899 (Bayer AG)

FARBENFABRIKEN vorm. FRIEDR. BAYER & Co
250 gr.
ELBERFELD.
ASPIRIN
Name gesetzlich geschützt in Deutschland und den meisten übrigen Industrieländern.
Registered in Germany and most of the other industrial countries.
Nom déposé en Allemagne et dans la plupart des autres pays industriels.

18 BMW

1916, Munich, Germany
Founder **Franz Josef Popp** Company **Bayerische Motoren Werke AG** HQ **Munich, Germany**
www.bmw.com

Left: Bavarian state flag
Right: Rapp logo

The Bayerische Motoren Werke GmbH (Bavarian Motor Works) was founded in 1917, following the reorganization of Bayerische Flugzeug Werke GmbH. Originally founded in 1916, this latter company was created in a merger between aircraft engine manufacturers Gustav Flugmaschinenfabrik and Rapp-Motorenwerke.

Showing the white and blue quadrants enclosed in a black circle bearing the company's initials, the famous BMW roundel evolved from the Rapp logo. However, where the Rapp logo used a horse as its symbol, BMW chose the chequered design of the Bavarian state flag.

After WWI, BMW stopped producing aircraft engines as agreed under the Treaty of Versailles, shifting its focus to motorcycles and automobiles.

The logo has stayed essentially the same for almost 100 years. Although the typography, the use of outlines and the size of the blue and white core changed a number of times, the logo needed only minor adjustments to stay up-to-date.

The year 2000 saw the latest change to a 3D representation of the roundel, just as if it was taken from the car's hood.

It's a widespread misconception that the logo symbolizes the movement of an aircraft propellor as seen in a 1929 advertisement. According to a BMW spokesman, even the company itself used to think the logo was tied to its aeronautical history.

The 1929 ad with propellor visual

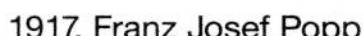
1917, Franz Josef Popp

1933

1951

1970

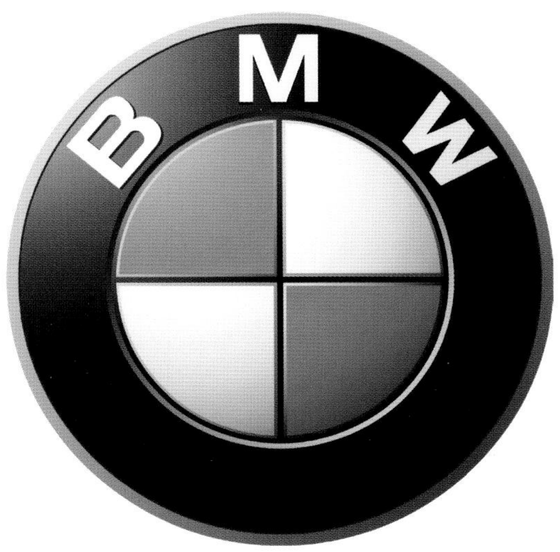

2000

77
BMW
MOTORRÄDER
BMW
BAYERISCHE MOTOREN WERKE AKTIENGESELLSCHAFT MÜNCHEN 46

'BMW motorcycles', poster, 1946
Opposite top: 'BMW 700', ad, 1960
Opposite below: BMW Z4M Coupé, 2006 (Ben Smith/Shutterstock.com)

Das ist Ihr Wagen:
Geräumiger Innenraum mit vier bequemen Sitzen · viel Platz für Gepäck · lebendiger, laufruhiger Viertaktmotor - 30 PS · vollsynchronisiertes Viergang-getriebe . . . und eine elegante, begeisternde Form -natürlich ein BMW 700
BMW 700

19 BP

1909, UK
Founder **William Knox D'Arcy**
Company **BP plc** HQ **London, UK**
www.bp.com

BP was founded as the Anglo-Persian Oil Company in 1909, when William Knox D'Arcy discovered oil in Persia (now Iran). The first BP 'motor spirit' ads appeared in automotive magazines around 1920.

An employee from the purchasing department, AR Saunders, won an in-house competition to design the first 'real' BP logo. He came up with the angular, serifed 'BP' with double quotation marks set in an outlined shield.

In the 1920s, the color of the shield varied between red, blue, green, black, yellow and white. In the 1930s, a request was sent out to all subsidiaries to consistently use green and yellow only in the brand. The reason for green and yellow is not entirely clear, but it was used first in France in 1923. In BP's home country of Britain, the first pumps and trucks were red, much to the dislike of certain people in the countryside who thought red spoiled the view.

In British ads, filling stations and garages, a patriotic 'BP' Union Jack logo was used to support the slogan "Buy British goods, BP: The British Petroleum".

After WWII, the shield was restyled in 1947, when the quotation marks were dropped and a black drop shadow was added to the lettering. After renaming the company from Anglo-Iranian Oil Company (1935) to British Petroleum Company in 1954, it was Raymond Loewy who simplified the logo four years later, losing the shield's outline and BP's drop shadow. He also made the letters rounder, which resulted in a cleaner and friendlier look.

Service man holding a can of Visco-Static Longlife oil, 1963

This logo also appeared enclosed in a heavy square outline. An updated logo was introduced in 1989, showing a contrasting shield outline and italicized lettering with softer, more subtle serifs.

In 2000, after the merger with American oil company Amoco, the BP logo had a complete makeover. 80 years after its introduction, the shield was replaced by the flower sunburst or *'helios'*, named after the Greek sun god. The *Helios* symbolized innovation, constant improvement, performance, vitality and environmental responsibility in an era when alternative energy sources were becoming increasingly important. The new strategy was captured in the added tagline 'Beyond Petroleum', not coincidentally synonymous with the company's initials. The company was renamed BP plc in 2001.

ca 1920

1920, AR Saunders

1922

1947

1958, Raymond Loewy

1989, Siegel & Gale

2000, Landor Associates

ITALIA

1 : 1.250.000

Above: BP ad with Union Jack logo, UK, 1922 (© BP plc)
Below: Plane being refueled with Air BP product, London City Airport, UK (© BP plc)
Opposite: BP road map of Italy, ca 1970

20 BRAUN

1921, Frankfurt am Main, Germany
Founder **Max Braun** Company **Braun GmbH** HQ **Kronberg, Germany**
www.braun.com

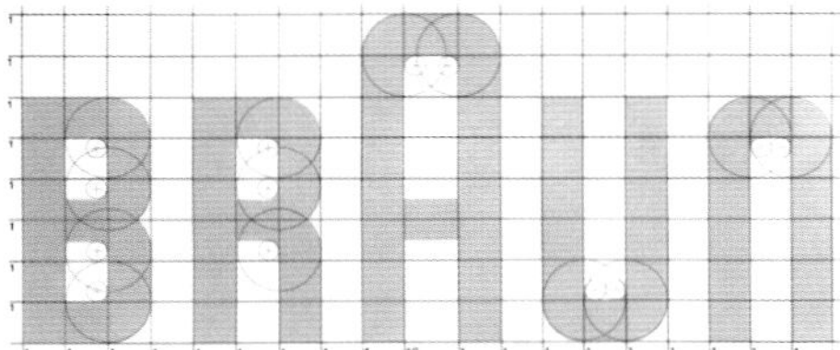

Design grid for the 1952 logo by Wolfgang Schmittel

Consumer electronics and appliances manufacturer Braun was founded by mechanical engineer Max Braun in Frankfurt in 1921. Initially making radio parts, by 1929 it also made complete power amplifiers and radio sets. The Braun logo with the distinctive raised 'A' in the middle was introduced in 1934.

After WWII, Braun became well known for its hi-fi audio and record players and the electric shaver. The products combined state-of-the-art technology with distinctive functional design. Dieter Rams, chief of design at Braun from 1961 to 1995 after joining the company in 1955, embodied Braun's philosophy when he coined the phrase "Less, but Better". Dieter Ram's designs revolutionized the design world and many of his original pieces now appear in museums.

Not long after sons Artur and Erwin took over the company management when Max Braun died suddenly in late 1951, the Braun logo was redesigned by Wolfgang Schmittel. In 1952, he joined the Braun design department as a freelancer. Upon his arrival, he constructed the logo based on a strict grid of squares and circles, but keeping the raised 'A'. It was part of the new design style, including the entire product line and all communications materials – from stationery and user instructions all the way to advertising.

The logo proved to be a timeless piece of design that would only be restyled once, when the letters became rounder, improving readability and giving the logo a friendlier look. Now part of Procter & Gamble, Braun is the global market leader in its core categories of foil shavers, epilators and hand blenders.

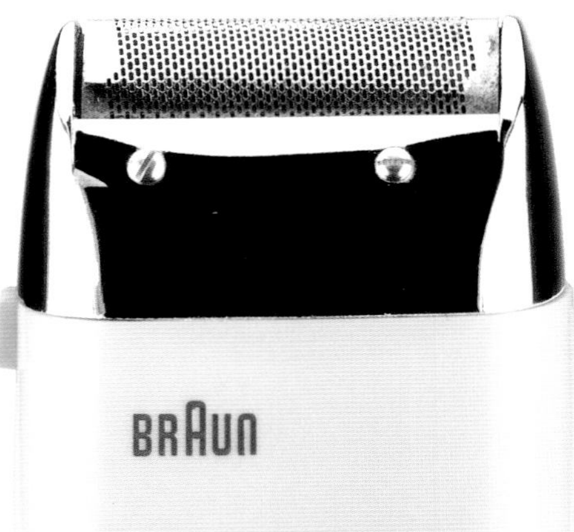

Electric shaver S60 by Dieter Rams, 1958

1934, Will Münch

1939

BRAUN

1952, Wolfgang Schmittel

BRAUN

1990s

21 BRITISH AIRWAYS

1919, London, UK
Founder **Aircraft Transport and Travel (AT&T)** Company **British Airways** HQ **London, UK**
www.ba.com

'Transfer at London Heathrow', baggage label, ca 1985

British Airways celebrated its 90th anniversary in 2009. BA's history can be traced back to Aircraft Transport and Travel, a company that carried its first international flight, to Paris, in November 1919.

In 1924, a merger between Instone, Handley Page Transport, The Daimler Airway and British Marine Air Navigation Company created Imperial Airways Ltd. The long-range air transport company adopted the 'Speedbird' logo in 1932.

The original British Airways, which resulted from a 1935 merger between a number of small UK air transport companies, was nationalized in 1939, joining forces with Imperial Airways to form the British Overseas Airways Corporation or BOAC. It continued to use the Speedbird as its symbol. The BOAC logotype had floating dots between the letters.

In 1965, the logotype was modernized and lost its dots. The Speedbird continued to be part of the logo.

Following an Act of Parliament, BOAC and BEA (British European Airways) merged to form British Airways in 1974. The typographic logo, in the British national colors, lost the Speedbird, although it could still be seen on the noses of the airplanes. In 1980, the livery changed to 'British' only.

With the privatization of BA, a new all-caps logo was launched in 1984, reintroducing the full name of the airline to all its planes. The line and sharp hook, called Speedwing, were derived from a combination of the British national flag, the Union Jack, and the Speedbird.

In 1997, the Speedwing evolved into a 3D flying ribbon, known as the Speedmarque. The new corporate identity was accompanied by a multitude of 'world image' tailfins to emphasize the company's international route network. Because the UK public missed its Union Jack, BA announced in 2001 that it would change all tailfins to the 'Chatham Dockyard Union Flag' of the Concorde.

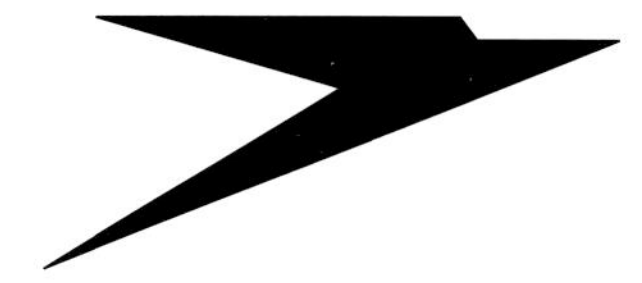

1932, Theyre Lee-Elliott

B·O·A·C

1940

1965

British
airways

1974

BRITISH AIRWAYS

1984, Landor Associates

1997, Newell and Sorrell

Heavy luggage label, ca 1979
Opposite top: British Airways Boeing 747, carrying the 'Chatham Dockyard Union Flag' on its tailfin (Eluveitie)
Opposite below left: BOAC timetable, 1958. Below right: 'Pleasure before business', ad, UK, 1960s

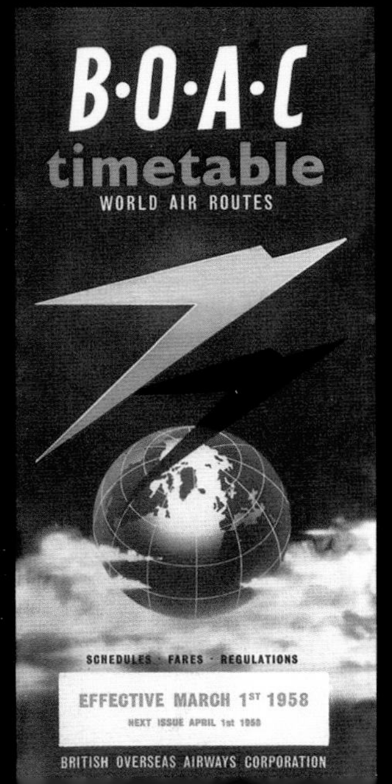
B·O·A·C
timetable
WORLD AIR ROUTES
SCHEDULES · FARES · REGULATIONS
EFFECTIVE MARCH 1ST 1958
NEXT ISSUE APRIL 1st 1958
BRITISH OVERSEAS AIRWAYS CORPORATION

Pleasure before business
BOAC
Fly VC10
To dream that you are floating high on a cotton wool cloud to North America can mean one of two things:
You have an excellent mattress.
You are in a BOAC VC10.
The BOAC VC10 is a dream aircraft. You sit up ahead of the jets, out of earshot from its great Rolls-Royce power. What you can hear, is yourself thinking that the luxurious BOAC seat is the ultimate in comfort.
The uncluttered wings give extraordinary lift so that the VC10 gets you off the ground 25% quicker than ordinary jets.
And it puts you gently down 20 mph slower. Altogether it's the most revolutionary jetliner that ever flew. Flights leave for North America all day, every day.
See your BOAC Travel Agent about them.
BOAC
takes good care of you

22 BURGER KING

1954, Miami, FL, USA
Founders **James McLamore, David R. Edgerton** Company **Burger King** HQ **Miami, FL, USA**
www.burgerking.com

Fast food chain Burger King was founded in 1954 in Florida. Sitting atop the sign in front of the first store in Miami, the 'Sitting King' logo made its debut in 1955. From 1960, the King character would play an important role in ads in TV commercials, both in animation and real life.

The original 'Bun Halves' logo debuted in 1969. Obviously created to signify the restaurant's association with hamburgers, it was a simple and effective logo with the brand name 'Burger King' in bulging red letters, representing the meat inside, sandwiched between two bun halves. This logo was restyled in 1994 by using a more regular, smoother font and different proportions for the bun halves and logotype. The top bun half was now bigger than the bottom one, representing the actual bun more accurately.

In a more radical update, after using the two Bun Halves logos for almost three decades, the 'Blue Crescent' logo was introduced in 1998. The bun halves were reduced in size but received gloss with highlight swooshes. Together with an updated type, it was wrapped in a prominent blue swirl and tilted on its axis, literally giving the logo a global feel.

Left: 'Where 60-second service begins', ad, USA, 1966
Right: 'New York loves burgers', ad, USA, 1977

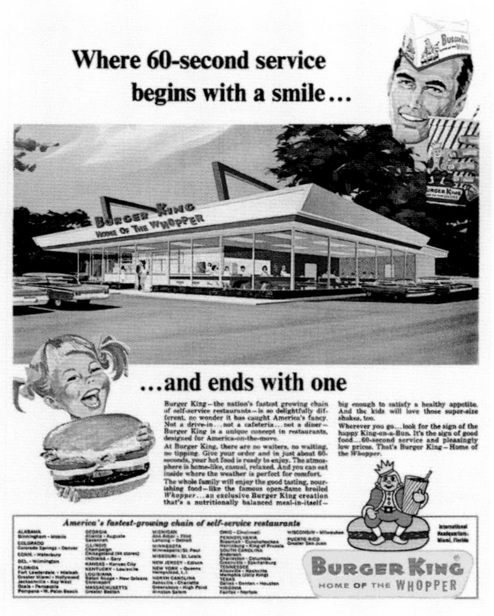

BurgerKing

1954

1955

1969

1994

1998, Sterling Brands

23 C&A

1841, Sneek, Netherlands
Founders **Clemens and August Brenninkmeijer**
Company **C&A Europe**
HQ **Vilvoorde, Begium and Düsseldorf, Germany**
www.c-and-a.com

The C&A fashion store chain was founded in 1841 as a textile company in the Dutch town of Sneek by two brothers, Clemens and August Brenninkmeijer, taking its company name from their initials. Originally from Germany, the Brenninkmeyer family had been trading in linen and textiles from their hometown in Mettingen since the 17th century. The first store opened twenty years after C&A was established.

In the first logo, 'C. en A. Brenninkmeijer' ('*en*' means 'and' in Dutch) is enclosed in a circle along with the store branch locations: Amsterdam, Groningen, Leeuwarden and Sneek. The brothers were clearly doing well.

As more and more C&A stores opened in the Netherlands and abroad, there was no longer room to mention all the cities in the logo. Consequently, they were dropped in 1912. Not long after, the circle morphed to an oval, and the famous wavy border was added in the 1920s. The border changed several times over the years, going from radiant and diagonally stripes to solid-color borders, and from a wavy shape to sharper 'flower petals' and back to wavy again. Meanwhile, the lettering changed marginally and the Dutch red, white and blue were introduced in 1958.

To celebrate the company's 170th anniversary in 2011, the inner oval, which had been blue with white lettering for over 50 years, changed the other way around to modernize the brand, resulting in a fresher and cleaner look.

Top right: C&A store, Duesseldorf, Germany, 1926 (C&A Europe)
Right: 'Beautiful...from C&A', poster, Netherlands, 2005

ca 1870

1912

1913

1920s

1947

1958

1984

1998

2005

2011, Saffron

24 CANON

1937, Tokyo, Japan
Founders **Takeshi Mitarai, Goro Yoshida, Saburo Uchida, Takeo Maeda**
Company **Canon Inc.** HQ **Tokyo, Japan**
www.canon.com

Kannon, the Buddhist Goddess of Mercy

The Seiki Kogaku Kenyusho company was founded in 1933 with the aim of producing world-class cameras. After trial and error, the first camera was introduced a year later: the Kwanon. The name was derived from the Buddhist goddess of mercy, Kannon, who is said to bestow favours in this world.

The goddess with the thousand arms was depicted in the first logo. The complex symbol was replaced by an italic script logotype that already showed some of the characteristics of the current logo. However, this logo was never released on the market.

After exceeding initial expectations, full-scale sales began in 1935. Around the same time, the company decided to change the brand name to Canon, a spelling that would be more accessible to a global market. The word Canon has a number of meanings, including 'sacred book', 'criterion' and 'standard'.

In 1953, the logo was fine-tuned to achieve a better overall balance. Finally, in 1956, after painstaking redesigning, Canon introduced the logo that the company uses to this day. It would become one of the longest-lived logos in the world.

Photojournalists at the UEFA Euro 2004 soccer tournament, Portugal, 2004

1934

1934

1935

Canon

1953

Canon

1956

25 CASTROL

1899, London, UK
Founder **Charles Cheers Wakefield** Parent Company **BP plc** HQ **London, UK**
www.castrol.com

On the 19th of March 1899, Charles 'Cheers' Wakefield set up an oil company called CC Wakefield & Co Ltd. Registered in 1909, the Wakefield Motor Oil 'Castrol' brand was a revolutionary series of lubricants for the new internal combustion engine, including cars, motorcycles, airplanes and race engines. The name 'Castrol' refers to the castor oil added to the blend to create a motor oil of a superior consistency.

Castrol products are still marketed under the red, white and green color scheme that dates back to the launch of Castrol motor oil in 1909. Until 1958, the Castrol brand logo was accompanied by 'Wakefield Motor Oil', and was shortened to just 'Motor Oil' in 1960 when the company name changed to Castrol Ltd.

Following Burmah Oil's acquisition of Castrol in 1966, the logo was updated when the new Castrol GTX launched in 1968. By this point, Castrol products were sold in more than 140 countries. Around 1980, a solid green square was added to create a stronger brand presence. The logo was also used in conjunction with a big Castrol logotype next to the green square.

In 2000, Burmah Oil and Castrol became part of the BP group. Castrol continued to lubricate engines under its own name. A new Castrol identity was unveiled in 2001 with more contemporary typography, taken out of the circle to improve readability. A 3D version of this logo was added in 2006.

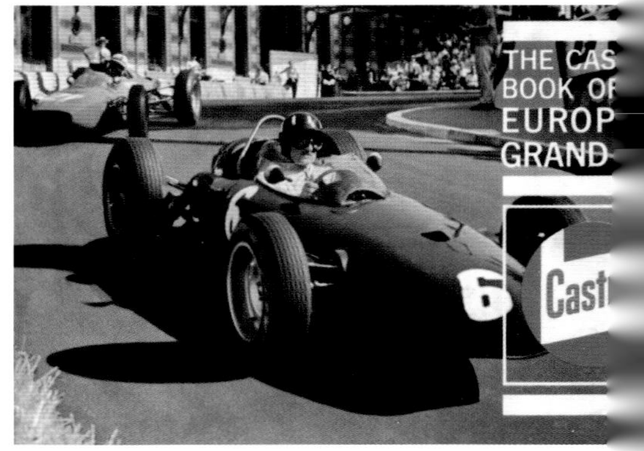

Top right: 'For champion performance...', ad, USA, 1958
Right: 'The Castrol book of the European Grand Prix, 1960s

1917

1929

1946

ca 1954

ca 1960

1968

ca 1980, Roger Clinton Smith

2001

2006

26 CHIQUITA

1899, Boston, USA
Founders **Minor C. Keith, Boston Fruit Company**
Company **Chiquita Brands** HQ **Cincinnati, OH, USA**
www.chiquita.com

Founded as the United Fruit Company, the company changed its name to Chiquita Brands International in 1990 after its famous brand of bananas, which was introduced in 1944. After a financial restructure in 2002, it was shortened to Chiquita Brands.

Much of the brand's fame should rightfully be credited to Miss Chiquita. The trademark logo was created by cartoonist Dik Browne, best known for 'Hägar the Horrible'. Originally only used in advertising, her presence was extended to a large branding program in 1963. The advertising campaign included affixing the trademark blue oval sticker to bananas.

'Help yourself-Havabanana!', ad, USA, ca 1950
Top right: Bunch of bananas with winning sticker designs, USA, 2010

Miss Chiquita became a real miss in the 1986 logo. The cartoony banana was replaced by a more mature and elegant Latina. Accompanied by a restyled logotype and the blue oval outline, the logo was ready to survive the next two decades.

The logo was restyled in 2010. Shown larger on the logo, Miss Chiquita subtly gained a few pounds, but her bigger smile made her seem happier than ever. The logotype was adapted to be more reminiscent of a bunch of bananas. Cutting through the yellow border, it gave the logo a better overall balance.

Chiquita recently held a public banana sticker contest in which 18 winners had a chance to showcase the versatile qualities of the banana. The blue oval and yellow border are recognizable enough to shine through, even in these alternative designs. Sadly available only in US grocery stores.

1944, Dik Browne

1961

1963

1986

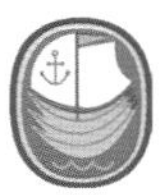

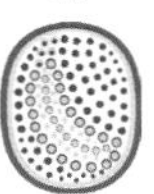

2010

27 CHUPA CHUPS

1958, Spain
Founder **Enric Bernat** Company **Chupa Chups S.A.U.** HQ **Barcelona, Spain**
www.chupachups.com

The first factory-produced lollipop was initially called the Chups, as suggested by an ad agency hired by founder Enric Bernat. The same agency also came up with a catchy radio jingle to market the Chups.

Spanish customers singing along with the jingle *'chupa chupa chupa un Chups'* ('lick, lick, lick a Chups') started to call the lollipop Chupa Chups. Inspired by its popularity, Enric Bernat decided to change the name to Chupa Chups. The logo evolved with the name, but the playfully informal style stayed the same.

After the Chupa Chups brand name was registered in 1962, the logo was redesigned. The new logo appeared on the packaging in 1963.

Above: Surrealist artist Salvador Dali designed the Chupa Chups logo in 1969
Right: Chupa Chups display, also known as 'The Wheel', 1999

As Chupa Chups became successful all over the world, a more creative design was warranted. Enric Bernat visited the renowned surrealist artist Salvador Dali, who sketched the daisy shape on a paper napkin in less than an hour. This new design fit perfectly on the crown of the wrapper. Up until then, the logo had been placed on the side of the lollipop, where it was difficult to read.

In 1978, two lollipops and a keyline were added to the logo, which was modernized again ten years later. The words 'Chupa' and 'Chups' now shared the same swirly font, while multiple colors were added to the keyline and the daisy. That logo serves the Chupa Chups to this day.

1958

1961

1963

1969, Salvador Dali

1978

1988, Landor Associates

CHUPA
Chups

This little girl was a familiar face in Chupa Chups' advertising during the 1960s

28 CITIBANK

1812, New York, NY, USA
Founder **Group of New York merchants** Company **Citibank** HQ **New York, NY, USA**
www.citigroup.com, online.citibank.com

Chartered by the New York State government, a group of merchants founded the City Bank of New York in 1812. It was the forerunner of Citibank, the international consumer bank of Citigroup. The logo depicted an eagle above a shield showing a windmill, symbolizing all directions of the wind, combined with different trading goods.

The logo changed when the bank joined the new national banking system of the USA in 1863, becoming the National City Bank of New York. The new name encircled a similar picture held by a native and 'new' American, and although it was restyled a few times, it served the bank for nearly 100 years. By 1870, the bank had become one of the largest banks in the country.

Following the merger with the First National Bank in 1955, the bank changed its name to the First National City Bank of New York, then shortened it to First National City Bank in 1962. A completely new logo was introduced with clear ties to the past, putting a compass inside a globe at the centre of the oval.

In 1968, the bank became a subsidiary of the newly formed one-bank holding company, First National City Corporation, which changed its name to Citicorp in 1974.

In 1976, First National City Bank changed its name to Citibank, which had been its informal nickname for some time. The simplified compass symbol was placed beside the prominent italicized logotype.

After announcing Citicorp's merger with insurance giant Travelers Group, forming Citigroup in 1998, Citigroup added the Travellers' red umbrella to a modernized logotype. After it was redesigned in 1999, the Citibank logo was based on the Interstate font, combining an abstract red umbrella with the word 'Citi' in bold letters, paired with the name of each Citigroup labels in a lighter version of the same font.

In 2005, the Citigroup logo was branded as Citi (after Travelers bought back the umbrella when it was divested in 2002). Officially keeping the Citigroup name, the logo used gray lettering and the same recognizable red arc for all its divisions. After years of acquisition, CitiGroup's goal was to better integrate the group's diverse parts into a more unified whole: "Our unified brand represents the promise to serve our clients as one company, as one Citi."

Citi logos at corporate level: 1974, 1976, 1998, 2005

1812

1863

1937

1955

1962

1976, Anspach Grossman Portugal

1999, Paula Scher, Pentagram

29 COCA-COLA

1886, Atlanta, GA, USA
Founder **John Pemberton** Company **The Coca-Cola Company** HQ **Atlanta, GA, USA**
www.coca-cola.com

What may well be the most famous logo in the world was designed by Dr. John Pemberton's bookkeeper, Frank Mason Robinson. Realizing that the two curly 'C's would look great in advertising, he came up with the name and flowing logotype in Spencerian script. The exact date is not clear, but the logo was registered as a trademark in 1887.

The Spencerian script was developed in the mid-19th century and was the dominant form of formal handwriting in the US during that period.

Prior to the scripted logo, at least one ad is known to have used the 1886 logo including the hyphen to improve readability. Several versions of the logo were used in the brand's very early days, due to the fact that a lot of the advertising material was hand-painted. The red and white color scheme was kept simple and distinctive to attract younger customers.

Above: Coca-Cola ad, USA, 1890s
Below: Coca-Cola truck, USA, 1930s
Next pages: 'Quality carries on', ad, USA, 1942

At the start of the 20th century, a more consistent image was developed, which resulted in the 1940s logotype. This version is still used today. However, many variations have been invented over the years for the support graphics, such as the shields, waves and taglines, with the aim of keeping the brand relevant. See the following pages for an overview.

COCA-COLA.

1886

ca 1887, Frank Mason Robinson

1893

ca 1900

ca 1940

1890s

1920s

1920s

1930s

1930s

1940s

1950s

1950s

1960s

Quality carries on

Coca-Cola
TRADE MARK REGISTERED
BOTTLE PAT. D-105529

5¢

Drink
Coca-Cola
TRADE-MARK REG. U.S. PAT. OFF.
Delicious and
Refreshing

'The Coke side of life', ad, 2009

1968, Lippincott & Margulies

1980s

1993

ca 1995

1998, Desgrippes Gobé & Associates

2001

2009, Turner Duckworth

2011

30 CREDIT SUISSE

1856, Zurich, Switzerland
Founder **Alfred Escher** Company **Credit Suisse Group AG** HQ **Zurich, Switzerland**
www.credit-suisse.com

Credit Suisse Group AG, the biggest Swiss bank in terms of market value, was founded by Alfred Escher in 1856 as the Schweizerische Kreditanstalt (Swiss Credit Bank) or SKA. Its first logo showed the initials in classical script lettering.

In 1930, a new SKA logo appeared. Resembling a coin, it bore twenty stars for the head office and 19 branch offices, surrounding the letters SKA and its founding date.

When the first foreign branch opened in New York City in 1940, a new logo was introduced. The simplified coin rim enclosed the abbreviations SKA, CS (Credit Suisse) and SCB (Swiss Credit Bank), encircling the founding date.

The image of the anchor was used to symbolize the tagline *'Verankert im Vertrauen'* ('Anchored in trust'), which was part of the 1952 logo. In a contest to design the company's new logo in 1968, the 'Wermelinger cross' was chosen as the winner. The black and white logo gained color in the 1976 restyling, when robust red and blue bars were added.

In 1978, the first collaboration between Credit Suisse and the First Boston Corporation was a fact. In 1990, CS acquired the US investment bank and was renamed CS First Boston.

In 1996, CS Holding became Credit Suisse Group, the holding company for Credit Suisse and Credit Suisse First Boston. Simplified logotypes were launched for both brands.

First Boston logos, 1932, 1990, 1996

To celebrate its 150th anniversary, a completely new logo was unveiled in 2006 to represent Credit Suisse as a single, integrated, global bank, uniting three divisions: investment banking, private banking and asset management. The name First Boston was dropped, but the two triangular shaped sails pulling the discrete logotype are based on the First Boston ship symbol.

Credit Suisse regional HQ at One Cabot Square, London, UK (Credit Suisse Group AG)

1856

1930

1940

1952

1968

1976

1996, Wolff Olins

CREDIT SUISSE

2006, Enterprise IG

31 DELTA

1928, Monroe, LA, USA
Founder **CE Woolman** Company **Delta Air Lines** HQ **Atlanta, GA, USA**
www.delta.com

The forerunner of Delta Airlines was Huff Daland Dusters Inc., founded in 1924, the first commercial agricultural flying company. C.E. Woolman, the principal founder of Delta Air Lines, bought Huff Daland Dusters and renamed the company Delta Air Service, for the Mississippi Delta region it served in 1928.

The first logo, nicknamed 'Huffer Puffer', featured Thor, the Norse god of thunder, war and agriculture. It symbolized the fight against the boll weevil infestation in the cotton fields. The triangular shield came from the Greek letter delta, or Δ.

In addition to mail services, Delta started operating passenger flights in 1929. The core values of speed, safety and comfort were referenced prominently in the logo.

The figure with the winged helmet is Mercury, the god of travel and commerce.

Lack of mail contracts forced the company to suspend passenger service. After the US Post Office assigned Air Mail Route 24 to Delta in 1934, it resumed passenger service, using a winged triangle inside a bigger triangle as its logo. It was soon replaced by a simplified version, often seen with 'AM 24' inside the triangle.

1945 saw the beginning of a whole series of 'Flying D' logos. Starting in 1947, they included a supporting oval in varying colors. A temporary addition of the abbreviation 'C&S' was due to the merger with Chicago & Southern Airlines in 1953. 'C&S' was removed from the slightly restyled logo again in 1955.

Left: Luggage label, USA, 1940s
Right: 'Merge to serve you better', ad, USA, 1953

1928

1929

ca 1934

1934

1945

1947

1953

1955

1959

1962

ca 1963

1987

1995, Landor Associates

2000, Landor Associates

2004

2007, Lippincott

The first red, white and blue triangle or 'widget' appeared in 1959, when Delta entered the jet era with the introduction of the DC-8's. It resembled the wings of a speeding jet seen overhead. The widget was used both pointing north and east. In the course of the 1960s, a number of variants of this logo appeared with 'Air Lines' in a smaller size to fit inside the supporting oval and circle.

Parallel to the acquisition of Western Airlines, a new serif typeface was used in 1987, keeping the widget. Again, in 1995, the typography was modified in an uppercase and lowercase two-tone version.

In 2000, the acute inner angle of the widget was replaced by a horizon curve and the name was shortened to just 'Delta' to celebrate the founding of the SkyTeam alliance. However, based on employee feedback, as well as nostalgia surrounding the 75th anniversary, the 'Heritage Widget' returned in 2004.

After a major company-wide reorganization, Delta unveiled a new logo in 2007. The shading gave the widget a three-dimensional impression. Together with a logotype recalling the 1960s, it reflected Delta's succesful transformation into a highly differentiated, customer-focused airline.

Above: Delta airplanes at Atlanta airport, ca 1970
Below: Current Delta 747-400 in flight (Delta Air Lines)

32 DEUTSCHE BANK

1870, Berlin, Germany
Founders **Adelbert Delbrück, Ludwig Bamberger**
Company **Deutsche Bank AG** HQ **Frankfurt am Main, Germany**
www.db.com

Deutsche Bank was named to reflect the bank's main focus on foreign trade, an area largely controlled by British and French banks. The German imperial eagle was portrayed in Deutsche Bank's first logo with a monogrammed shield on its chest.

The merger of Deutsche Bank and Disconto-Gesellschaft in October 1929 was the largest merger to date in the German banking industry. A cleaner, simplified eagle was adopted. Soon after, in the mid-1930s, the Deutsche Bank decided to use initials enclosed by an oval for its logo, inspired by the Disconto-Gesellschaft logo.

In post-WWII reorganizations in 1947-48, Deutsche Bank was split into ten autonomous regional institutions. Although they were not allowed to bear the DB name, the regional logos used the style of the encircled initials.

When these regional banks were combined into just three successor institutions in 1952, the logos were redesigned to resemble stylized coin rims. Finally, when the regional banks were merged into a single bank again in 1957, with its head office in Frankfurt am Main, the pre-war logo was reintroduced.

In 1973, the bank invited eight designers to submit concepts for a new visual identity. An independent jury choose Anton Stankowski's Constructivist-style enclosed 'forward slash' (one of his eight ideas). In its annual report the bank said, "By virtue of its relative simplicity, the new design is both extremely eye-catching and easy to remember. The square framework can be regarded as symbolizing security and the upward stroke as portraying dynamic development." The entry showed the symbol on its own, but the Univers set logotype was added afterwards.

Having grown into one of the strongest and most recognized symbols in the world, Deutsche Bank opted for a new brand and visual identity in which the symbol functions on its own. Anton Stankowski got his way eventually.

Deutsche Bank HQ, Frankfurt am Main, Germany
(Jürgen Matern)

1870

until 1929 *(Disconto-Gesellschaft)*

1929

mid 1930s

1947

1952

1957

1974, Anton Stankowski

2011, 2br

33 DR. OETKER

1891, Bielefeld, Germany
Founder **Dr. August Oetker** Company **Dr. August Oetker KG** HQ **Bielefeld, Germany**
www.oetker.com

The German branded food company was founded by pharmacist Dr. August Oetker in 1891. He developed Germany's first storable and tasteless baking powder. 'Backin' revolutionized baking thanks to its guarantee of perfect results and its high quality. When Dr. Oetker acquired the Aschoff Pharmacy in Bielefeld, he also took over its trademark with the goblet and foaming mineral water.

Dr. Oetker was unhappy with the pharmacy's original logo. He came up with the concept of *'Ein heller Kopf'* (which translates as 'a clear head', but also means a bright mind) and decided to visualize the slogan. As he put it, "In a fortuitous moment, I had the idea of using the slogan '*Ein heller kopf*' in my ads, visualized as a white silhouette of a woman's head against a dark background."

He therefore held a contest in 1899, which was won by Theodor Kind. Kind used his daughter Johanna and her fashionably large hair knot to model for the profiled silhouette. The 'Hellkopf' logo was registered in 1899, and variations on this theme were used until the 1920s. Some showed two silhouettes with a goblet in between, while others used only one silhouette. In addition, the silhouette was used in a variety of rectangular backgrounds, which were later replaced by an oval. A 1927 version showed a restyled oval with a curved border and a hairstyle that was adapted to 1920s fashions, as well as the choice of red to be used for all communication.

Top right: 'A bright head uses Dr. Oetker products only', newspaper ad, 1899, Germany (© Dr. August Oetker KG)
Right: 'Dr. Oetker cake, child's play to bake', ca 1915 (© Dr. August Oetker KG)

1891

1902

1899, 1899, 1899, 1909

1910, 1910, 1912, 1914

1914

1927

Starting in 1956, the oval was joined by the logotype in a bold sans serif enclosed in a pentagon, increasing the impact of the packaging. Where the pentagon was variable in color depending on the product, the oval stayed in the company's familiar red.

The final version of Dr. Oetker's oval was unveiled in 1969 and is still in use today. The color red was made more dominant by transforming the pentagon into a red outlined oval shape which enclosed the blue logotype and Johanna's oval.

The 'Competent Lines' that anchor the logo in the upper left corner were added in 1986 for better recognition of the Dr. Oetker products on supermarket shelves. These lines were slightly restyled in 1997.

'Every Sunday a cake - self baked with Backin', ad for 'Backin' baking powder, Germany, 1959
(© Dr. August Oetker KG)

Series of packaging for cupcake mixes and decorations by Sogood, Netherlands, 2011

1927

1956

1969

1986

1997

34 DUNKIN' DONUTS

1950, Quincy, MA, USA
Founder **William Rosenberg** Parent Company **Dunkin' Brands** HQ **Canton, MA, USA**
www.dunkindonuts.com

Family snapshot, USA, 1970s (edcleve)
Below right: 'America runs on Dunkin', 2006

The first Dunkin' Donuts logo featured 'Dunkie', a cheerful character serving coffee and donuts supported by a bold script logotype. The logo used on road signs was different, however, with the two stacked words in all capitals.

The second-generation logo is actually a combination of logo elements: the stacked brand name, the brand name as a typographic donut, and the coffee mug. All elements could be combined or used separately as needed.

The donut and mug symbol was later simplified to a purely graphic element. The brand name took on the curves of the donut itself, creating a famous logotype so recognizable that it was eventually used on its own.

In 1980, industrial designer Lucia N. DeRespinis at Sangren & Murtha walked into the graphic design department and wondered why all the logo designs were in toasty browns. She suggested keeping the logotype, but in her daughters' favorite colors of orange and pink, which she also used in the prototype interior for Dunkin' Donuts. "Donuts are fun and celebratory", she said; the client couldn't agree more.

The coffee cup symbol reappeared in 2002, now steaming. "While coffee and donuts are core to our business, neither stands alone," said Ken Kimmel, vice president of Dunkin' Donuts Concepts. "The addition of a steaming coffee cup to the logo supports our belief that coffee and donuts go hand-in-hand. Donuts is in our name, but we also serve more than 2 million cups of consistently delicious coffee per day."

Only two years later in 2004, a more streamlined version of the coffee cup appeared, showing the 'DD' abbreviation for better readability and use of a third color.

1950

DUNKIN'
DONUTS

(road sign logo)

ca 1965

ca 1975

1980, Lucia N. DeRespinis, Sangren & Murtha

2002, Design Forum

2004

35 FEDEX

1973, Litlle Rock, AR, USA
Founder **Frederick W. Smith** Company **FedEx Corporation** HQ **Memphis, TN, USA**
www.fedex.com

In 1971, Frederick W. Smith bought a controlling interest in Arkansas Aviation Sales, based in Little Rock, Arkansas. When it proved difficult to get airfreight delivered quickly, he redesigned the distribution system, incorporated the company, and officially began operations in April 1973, using 14 airplanes from Memphis International Airport under the name Federal Express.

'Federal' suggested nationwide service. Smith hoped to obtain a contract with the Federal Reserve Bank, although it did not materialize, and believed the name was good for attracting public attention. The first logo consisted of an all-caps Federal Express placed diagonally in white and red in a purple and white rectangle.

In 1994, the strategic opportunity arose to position the company as the industry's global leader. Widely nicknamed FedEx, the company decided to officially adopt the abbreviation. Based on a mix of Univers and Futura, the new logo was deceptively simple, cleverly holding a right-pointing arrow in the space between the 'E' and 'x'. To strongly communicate the new strategy, the tagline "The World On Time" was introduced.

In 1998, FedEx acquired the logistics businesses of Caliber System Inc. to form FDX Corporation. It also meant the beginning of a two-year rebranding operation which made it easy for customers to understand the global scope of Fedex and its range of services.

At a corporate level, FDX was renamed FedEx Corporation (in purple-grey). Business units were divided into companies that operate independently yet compete collectively. They were color-coded to express service specializations like FedEx Express (purple-orange), FedEx Ground (purple-green), FedEx Freight (purple-red), FedEx Custom Critical (purple-blue) and FedEx Trade Networks (purple-yellow). The cleaner-looking sans serif descriptors in Univers debuted in 2006.

FedEx and its operating companies, 2008 (FedEx Corporation)

1973, Richard Runyan

1994, Lindon Leader, Landor Associates

2000, Landor Associates

2006, Landor Associates

36 FIAT

1899, Turin, Italy
Founder **Giovanni Agnelli** Company **Fiat S.p.A.** HQ **Turin, Italy**
www.fiat.com

First Fiat logo used in print, Italy, 1899

The Fabbrica Italiana di Automobili Torino, better known as Fiat, was founded in 1899 in Turin, Italy. The first factory opened a year later.

A collection of car badges reveals the logo's history, but the first Fiat logo in print was a representation of an old paper scroll with the abbreviation F.I.A.T. The paper scroll idea was also used for the first car badge, using the company's full name and car production number.

The characteristic Fiat logotype with the backslanting upper part of the 'A' was first used in 1901, when the company decided to use a 'proper' logo, surrounded by Art Nouveau floral motifs and a rising sun.

Giovanni Agnelli, recognized for his determination and strategic vision, became the Managing Director of the company in 1902. He adopted the oval Fiat logo in 1904. Again, Art Nouveau decorations surrounded the blue rectangle.

After WWI, Fiat started to develop affordable cars in mass production. In 1921, the simplified logo became circular, with the Fiat name in red on a white background. The stylized laurel wreath celebrated Fiat's victories in the first competitive motor races.

In the 1930s, the circle evolved into a rectangular shape which eventually took the form of a shield, which fit better on the front grills on the new models. With a series of slight variations, these logos were used on Fiat cars up until 1965. A circular logo was also reintroduced briefly.

Italy saw a major economic boom in the late 1950s and 1960s, with the automotive sector as the 'engine' driving the economy. Production grew rapidly through increased automation of the manufacturing processes. The logo was modernized in 1968, featuring four blue rhombuses. The logo was the main identifier for the entire Fiat group.

By 1993, the car division of the company, Fiat Auto S.p.A., included the brands Fiat, Lancia, Abarth, Autobianchi, Ferrari, Alfa Romeo and Maserati.

A new Fiat logo debuted in 1999 to celebrate the company's 100th anniversary. The centenary trademark returned to the round design dating from the 1920s, and included the laurels and speckled blue background.

The latest logo was launched on the 2007 Fiat Bravo. It is a marriage of the famous red shield shape that graced Fiat cars between the 1930s and 1960s on the one hand and the circular logos of the 1920s on the other. Fiat returned to the company's original mission, namely "to build cars with attractive styling and exciting engines, cars that are accessible and improve the quality of everyday life."

1899

1901

1904, Carlo Biscaretti

1921

1925

1929

1931

1931

1932

1938

1959

1965

1968

1999

2007, Robilant Associati

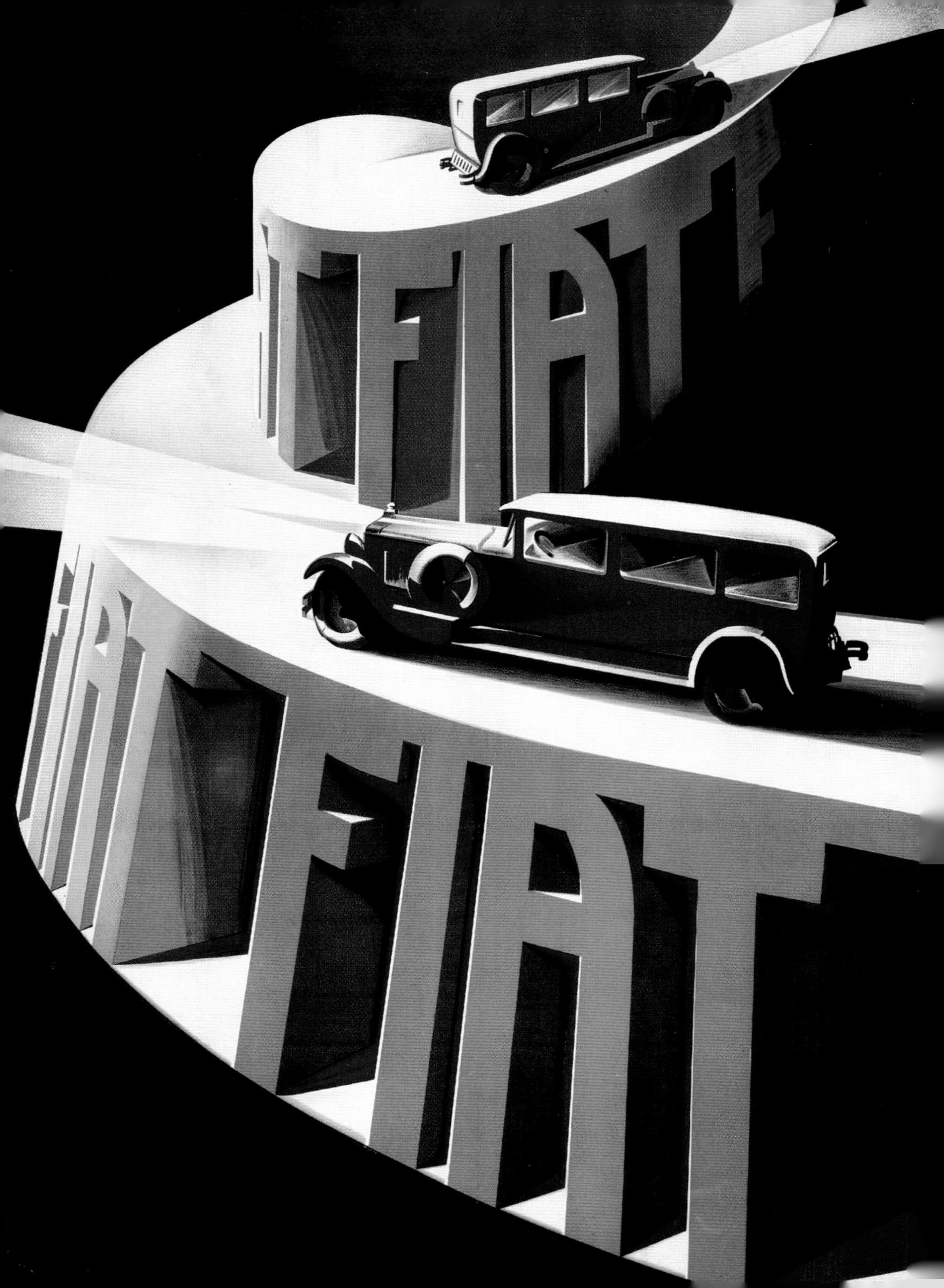
FIAT
FIAT

Opposite: Fiat poster featuring the 520S by Giuseppe Riccobaldi, Italy, 1928

Right: Fiat 125 owner's manual, Netherlands, 1970
Below: Fiat 500C, 2009

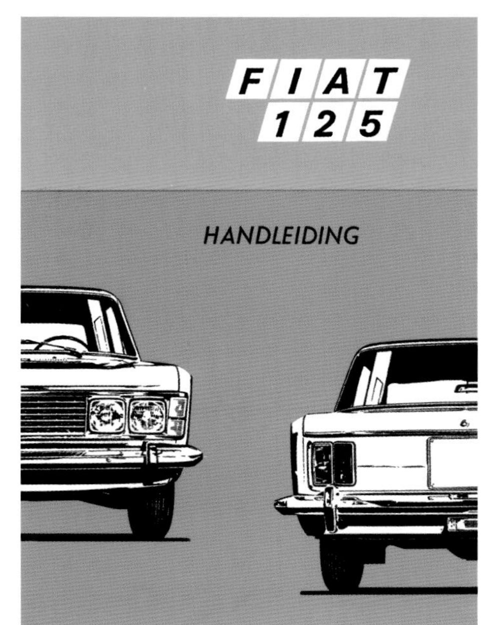

37 FISHER-PRICE

1930, East Aurora, NY, USA
Founders **Herman Guy Fisher, Irving R. Price, Margaret Evans Price, Helen M. Schelle**
Parent Company **Mattel** HQ **East Aurora, NY, USA**
www.fisher-price.com

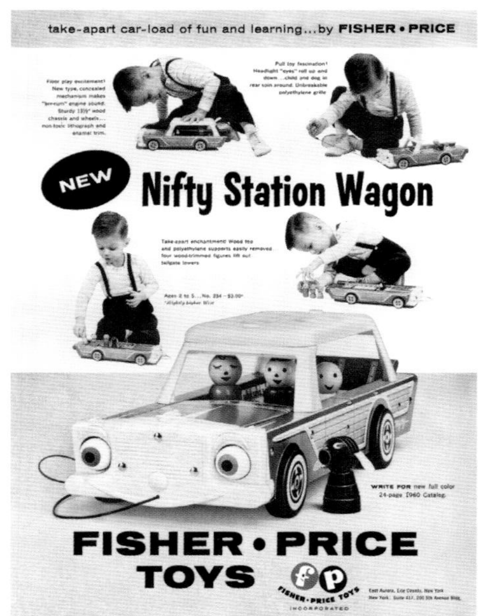

'Nifty Station Wagon', ad, USA, 1960
Right: 'Laugh & Learn Cookie Shape', baby toy, 2011

The name of toy manufacturer Fisher-Price was a combination of two of the three founders' surnames. Toy production, using extremely durable materials like steel and ponderosa pine, was based on the principles of intrinsic play value, ingenuity, strong construction, and value for money, which were represented in the first logo. The city of manufacture was also included in the logo, as was common in those times.

In 1956, Fisher-Price started producing its toys from a new, cheaper and fashionable material. It was the era of plastic. Plastic was also ideal for very brightly colored decorations that lasted longer. The logo changed drastically, with the playful initials in primary colors as its focal point. By simply adding a dot and a curved line, the 'f' was transformed into a smiling face with a funny hat, raising the fun level.

The 1957 restyled version, with the two balls and the word 'toys' back in, evolved into the famous 'gift-tag' logo of 1962. It adorned all packaging for twenty years, during which a number of different typefaces for the brand name were used.

By 1982, the logo had been distilled to the company name. Although the red awning had been part of Fisher-Price packaging design since the late 1950s, it was only integrated into the logo in 1992. Following the brand's acquisition by Mattel, the logo changed again in 1994, when the brand name was placed inside the red awning.

1931

1956

1957

1962

Fisher-Price

1982

1992

1994

38 FORD

1903, Detroit, MI, USA
Founder **Henry Ford** Company **Ford Motor Company**
HQ **Dearborn, MI, USA**
www.ford.com

In need of capital to continue manufacturing cars, the Ford Motor Company, previously called Ford & Malcomson Ltd., was incorporated in 1903, with founder Henry Ford himself owning 25.5% of the company. The full company name and Detroit as the place of manufacture are shown enclosed by an Art Nouveau oval frame in the first logo.

The Ford script is credited to Childe Harold Wills, Ford's first chief engineer and designer, who had made something similar for his business card. Several versions of the logotype appeared during the following years, some also including support graphics. The most significant one would be the bird-shaped version of 1912. The first ovals also appeared in 1912, but it would be years before the famous blue version came around.

The 'Blue Oval' eventually debuted in 1928, with the launch of the Model A. It set the basic shape and color of future Ford logos, although it was rounder than its current iteration. The company has experimented with different width-to-height ratios, and even opted for a rounded diamond shape in 1957.

The last major change to the logo was made around 1960. Today, the framing shape has evolved into an oval with a width-to-height ratio of 8:3. The current 'Centennial Blue Oval', which lost the chrome frame from 1976, was introduced in 2003 as part of the 100th anniversary of Ford Motor Company.

IDEALLY ADAPTED
FOR A WOMAN'S PERSONAL USE

The woman who has many demands on her time requires a car on which she can always depend for timely use. It must be handled easily; it must assure her of instant and unfailing control; and it must be both good-looking and comfortable —ready for strenuous wear and service. Above all, it must possess the prestige of high success in the motor world. These demands explain why so many thousands of women drive Fords.

TUDOR SEDAN, $590 - - FORDOR SEDAN, $685 - - COUPE, $525
[All prices f. o. b. Detroit]

CLOSED CARS

Striking Power!

Cobra-429 Drag Pack

Cobra's the one. A 429 CID V-8's the standard engine; 360 is the standard horsepower. Ford's great, butter-smooth 4-speed box with Hurst Shifter* is standard too. And for serious drag people, we've got the real earth shaker. Cobra Jet 429 Ram-Air V-8 with Drag Pack. It's got 11.0:1 compression, heavy-duty con rods and mains, a high riser intake manifold and header type exhausts. The 700 cfm 4-barrel carb breathes in from a through-the-hood shaker scoop. Then comes the drag pack: Traction-Lok Differential with 3.91 or 4.30:1 ratio, engine oil cooler, forged aluminum pistons and 4-bolt center main bearings. All this lean muscle is controlled by Cobra's competition suspension. It's nailed to the pavement with 7" rim wheels and F70 x 14 wide-tread glass belts. So get yourself a Big Snake and strike.

P.S.: If you've already got a Ford Stocker and you want to turn it into a real screamer, do your own thing with Ford MUSCLE PARTS. You'll find 'em in your Ford Dealer's Performance Corner.

Ford Power turns it on!

For the full story on all the performance Fords for 1970, visit your Ford Dealer and get our big 16-page 1970 Performance Digest. Or write to:

FORD PERFORMANCE DIGEST, Dept. CC-10, P.O. Box 747, Dearborn, Michigan 48121.

COBRA

Top right: 'Ideally adapted for a woman's personal use', ad, 1924
Right: 'Striking power', ad for Ford Cobra, USA, 1970

1903

1907, Childe Harold Wills

ca 1910

1912

1912

1928

1957

ca 1960

1976

2003

Ford
U.S.A.
85

Some Ford Advantages for 1941:

NEW ROOMINESS. Bodies are longer and wider this year, adding as much as seven inches to seating width.

SOFT, QUIET RIDE. A new Ford ride, with new frame and stabilizer, softer springs, improved shock absorbers.

GREAT POWER WITH ECONOMY. Ford cars are the most powerful in their price field, and hold records for economy as well as for performance.

BIG WINDOWS. Windshield and windows increased all around to give nearly four square feet of added vision area in each '41 Ford Sedan.

LARGEST HYDRAULIC BRAKES in the Ford price field, give added safety, longer brake-lining wear.

GET THE FACTS AND YOU'LL GET A FORD!

Above: 'Get the facts and you'll get a Ford', ad, USA, 1941
Below: Front grill of a Ford F-series Super Duty, 2011
Opposite: Ford V8 Cabriolet front grill car badge, 1937

39 FUJIFILM

1934, Japan
Founder **Government of Japan** Company **Fujifilm Holdings Corporation** HQ **Tokyo, Japan**
www.fujifilm.com

Fuji Photo Film Co., Ltd. was founded based on a government plan to establish a domestic photographic film manufacturing industry. Its first logo depicted Mount Fuji and exotic curly lettering enclosed in a circle, symbolizing Japan's rising sun.

As the brand shifted to a more international focus, the logo was changed. In 1960, the logo was still related to the rising sun, this time transformed into an oval. With the addition of 'film' in the bold sans serif typography and the national color red, it was a dramatic change.

What may well be the most famous Fuji logo appeared in 1980. The letters were cleverly assembled to form a red chip that looks three-dimensional. This logo would serve the company until 2006. However, from 1985 on, it was accompanied by the full brand name: Fuji Film. First written as two separate words, it became one word after 1992.

In October 2006, the Fujifilm Group shifted to a new group management structure as 'FUJIFILM Holdings Corporation'. This called for a new logo. The red element (the dot on the 'i') in the center of the logo is meant to symbolize the company's commitment to cutting-edge technology.

GET
THE TRUE PICTURE
OF A BIG MOMENT. FUJI-SHARP!
Only FUJICOLOR HR
gives you super-sharp images; extra-fine grain;
subtlest tones and textures; richest colours...
BECAUSE of the extraordinary HR emulsion technique
developed by FUJI to make FUJICOLOR HR
a high resolution film no one else can match for clarity.
So sharpen up your pictures. And shoot with
FUJICOLOR HR to GET THE TRUE PICTURE.
FUJI PHOTO FILM CANADA INC
FUJI FUJICOLOR HR

Top right: 'Get the true picture', ad, Canada, ca 1985
Right: Fujifilm compact camera Finepix XP20, 2010

Although green is an important corporate color for Fujifilm, it has never been part of the logo.

1934

1960

1980, Landor Associates

ca 1985

1992

FUJIFILM

2006

40 GAP

1969, San Francisco, CA, USA
Founders **Donald Fisher, Doris Fisher**
Company **The Gap, Inc** HQ **San Francisco, CA, USA**
www.gap.com

This American clothing retailer chose its name based on the 'generation gap', targeting a young clientele when it first started in 1969. The original Gap logo was a trademark used on retail apparel. From 1974, it was also a private label. The characteristic angle could be used for either 'the' or 'gap', depending on which seemed most appropriate in any given situation, although there are examples where both words are horizontal.

Updating its style to suit the changing times, the Gap introduced the blue square in the 1980s. In this version, the logotype was given stylishly slim serif caps in Spire Regular. The wide letterspacing was typical of the 80s.

In October 2010, Gap introduced a new logo in an attempt to create a more contemporary look for the retail market, limiting its initial launch to the US. After over 25 years, updating the logo seemed only logical. But the new logo reduced the now-iconic blue box to a background shape hidden behind a relatively bold Helvetica typeface.

In response to the resulting public outcry, the company returned to its 'blue box' logo only a few days later, leaving the rest of the world practically unaware of the incident. The Gap had learned its lesson the hard way: the company may think it owns the logo, but the public has the final say.

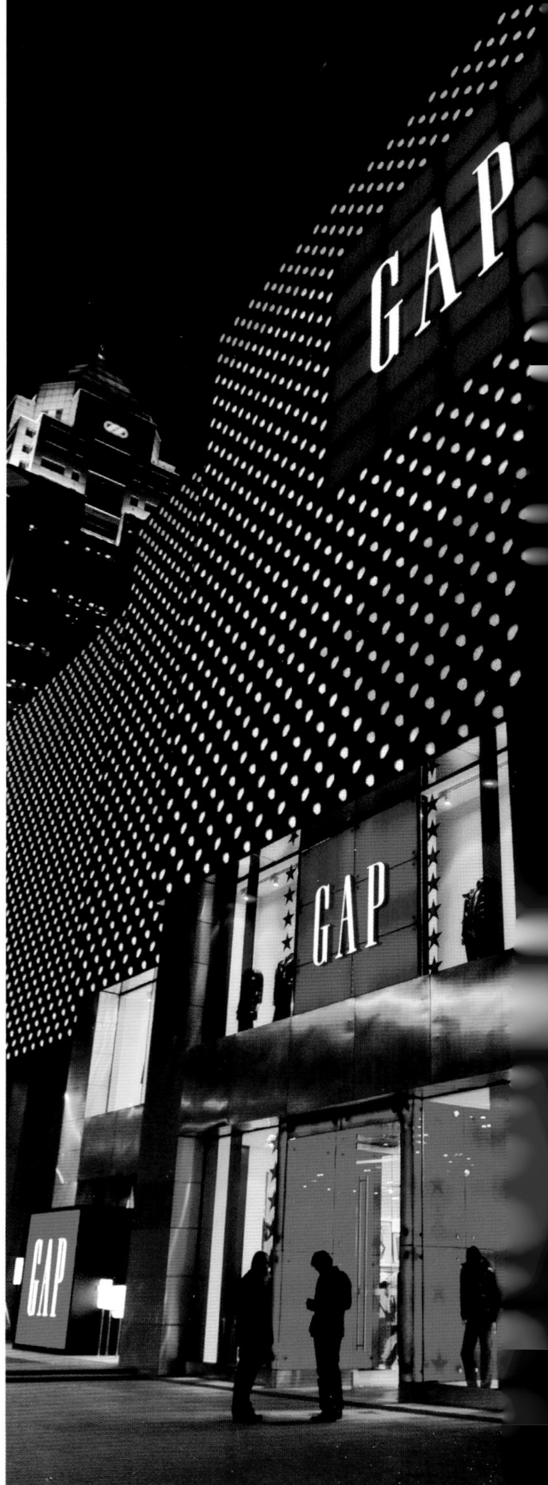

GAP Store, Shanghai, China, 2010 (Simon Q)

1969

1984

2010, Laird & Partners

2010

41 GOODYEAR

1898, Akron, OH, USA
Founder **Frank Seiberling** Company **Goodyear Tire & Rubber Company** HQ **Akron, OH, USA**
www.goodyear.com

The Goodyear Tire & Rubber Company was founded in 1898 by 38-year-old Frank Seiberling. In its early years, Goodyear produced horseshoe pads, bicycle and carriage tires, fire hoses and even rubber poker chips. It is currently the largest rubber company in the world.

The company was named in honour of Charles Goodyear, who had died broke in 1860 despite his discovery of vulcanization in 1839, after many years of experimentation. This technology used heat and sulfur to weatherproof rubber. Until then, rubber had been vulnerable to changing temperatures, freezing hard in winter and turning soft and sticky in summer.

In his own words, "Life should not be estimated exclusively by the standard of dollars and cents. I am not disposed to complain that I have planted and others have gathered the fruits. A man has cause for regret only when he sows and no one reaps."

Seiberling derived his inspiration for the 1901 winged-foot logo from his own newel-post statuette of the Roman god Mercury.
This association with the swift messenger of good news for all the gods of mythology added a feel of speed and positivity.

It is remarkable how little the logo changed over time, despite a number of adjustments in typography, shading, and slant of the lettering. It is still going strong after 110 years.

'More people ride on Goodyear tires', ad, USA, 1936

1901

1919

ca 1929

1930s

1950s

ca 1955 *(road sign)*

ca 1960 *(road sign)*

ca 1970

AKRON
SANTA CLAUS
PILGRIM

Goodyear has been using blimps since 1912. The company even acquired Zeppelin patents in 1924 to construct the first rigid airships in the US and was contracted by the US Navy to build airships in 1928. Goodyear still uses blimps for advertising purposes. This photo shows the 'The Pilgrim', the company's first public relations blimp dressed up as the Santa Claus Express for the occasion, ca 1928 *(Goodyear Tire & Rubber Company)*

42 GOOGLE

1998, Mountain View, CA, USA
Founders **Larry Page, Sergey Brin** Company **Google Inc** HQ **Mountain View, CA, USA**
www.google.com

Best known for its popular search engine, Google was founded by Stanford University students Larry Page and Sergey Brin in 1998.

The name of the company is derived from the word 'googol', a mathematical term for the number that is represented by the numeral one followed by 100 zeros. It reflected the seemingly infinite amount of information on the web. Google's predecessor in 1996, known as Backrub, used a logo that depicted Larry Page's own hand.

Several 'primitive' logos were created before the company was founded, including the 1997 example shown here. Co-founder Sergey Brin created the first official Google logo in 1998 using GIMP, a graphics editing program. An exclamation mark was added a few months later, inspired by the Yahoo! logo.

A new, more mature logo based on Gustav Jaeger's Catull typeface was introduced in 1999. The exclamation mark was removed. The logo was not restyled again until late in 2009, with an official introduction in 2010. Based on the same typeface and colors, it features a much more sophisticated and subtle use of letter shading and dropshadows.

From 1998, Google has included what are known as Google Doodle logos, decorative variations on the Google logo to celebrate holidays, anniversaries, and the lives of famous artists and scientists. It made searching on Google more fun for its users worldwide. The Doodles have become very popular over the years, expressing Google's creative and innovative nature. More than 1000 Doodles were created; the following pages show a small selection.

Google search page, Netherlands, 2009

1996 *(BackRub)*

1997

Google

Google!

1998, Sergey Brin

1998, Sergey Brin

Google

1999, Ruth Kedar

Google

2010, Ruth Kedar

Opposite page:

1 40th anniversary of Sesame Street, selected countries, 2009
2 Michelangelo's birthday, global, 2003
3 Australia Day, Australia, 2005
4 Happy Halloween, US, 2005
5 Torino Olympic Games, global, 2006
6 Seasonal holidays, global, 2007
7 Earth Day, global, 2008
8 50th anniversary of the Lego brick, global, 2008
9 First day of summer, 2008
10 Happy Halloween, selected countries, 2009
11 Loy Krathong, Thailand, 2009
12 Bastille Day, France, 2002
13 Happy Valentine's Day, global, 2003
14 Teacher's Day, China, 2005
15 Vincent Van Gogh's birthday, global, 2005
16 Sir Arthur Conan Doyle's birthday, global, 2006
17 Happy Valentine's Day, global, 2007
18 Piet Mondriaan's birthday, global, 2002
19 Charles Rennie Mackintosh's birthday, UK, 2008
20 Tomato Festival, Spain, 2008
21 Birthday of Constantin Brancusi, selected countries, 2011
22 Isamu Noguchi's Birthday, Japan, 2009
23 St. George's Day, UK, 2002
24 Happy Father's Day, global, 2004
25 Leonardo Da Vinci's birthday, global, 2005
26 Google 8th Anniversary, global, 2006
27 Women's Day, selected countries, 2011
28 Anniversary of the first film projection, Spain, 2008
29 Happy Holidays from Google, global, 2008
30 Queen's Day, Netherlands, 2008
31 St. Patrick's Day, US, 2004
32 Happy St. Patrick's Day! (Doodle designed by Doodle 4 Google Ireland winner Evan O'Sullivan Glynn), 2009
33 50th Anniversary of Sandmännchen, Germany, 2009
34 US Elections, US, 2004
35 Andy Warhol's Birthday, global, 2002
36 50th anniversary of the discovery of DNA structure, global, 2003
37 Louis Braille's Birthday, global, 2006
38 Countdown to Beijing Olympic Games, China, 2007
39 iGoogle Artist Themes designed by Jeff Koons, global, 2008
40 Independence Day, US, 2008
41 First Day of Spring, 2008
42 Brazil wins bid for 2016 Olympics, Brazil, 2009
43 Mahatma Gandhi's Birthday, selected countries, 2009
44 St. Andrew's Day, UK, 2009

This page:

45 Anniversary of the first ascent of Mount Everest, global, 2008
46 Anniversary of discovery of X-Rays, global, 2010
47 Crop circles, selected countries, 2009
48 Comic-Con, design and pencil Jim Lee, ink by Scott Williams, and color by Alex Sinclair (DC Comics), US, 2009
49 Alfons Mucha's 150th birthday, selected countries, 2010
50 Frank Lloyd Wright, global, 2005

45

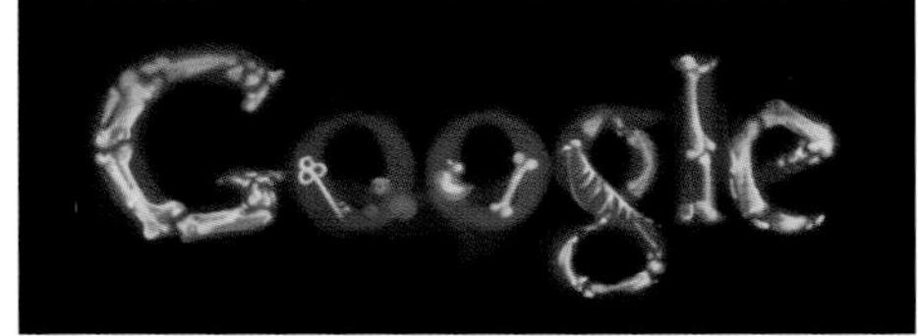

46

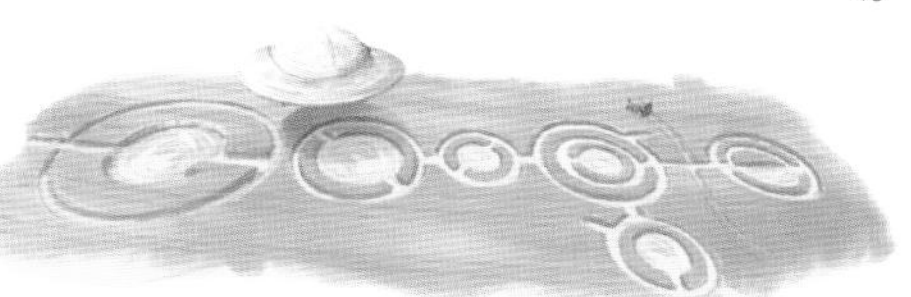

47

48

49

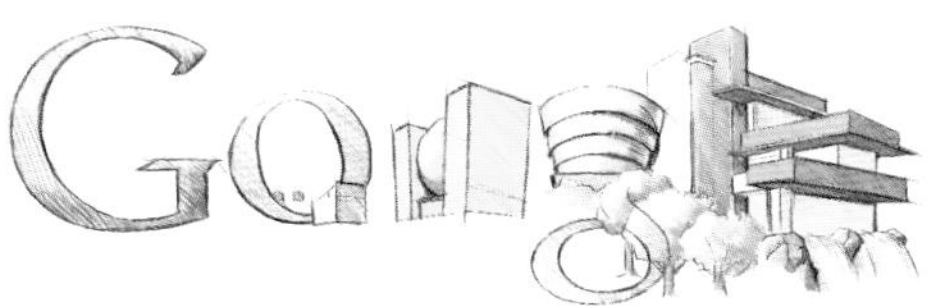

50

43 HERTZ

1918, Chicago, IL, USA
Founder **Walter L. Jacobs** Company **Hertz Corporation** HQ **Park Ridge, NJ, USA**
www.hertz.com

The small company founded by Walter Jacobs was initially known as Rent-a-Car Inc. until its acquisition in 1923 by John Hertz, president of Yellow Cab and Yellow Coach and Truck Manufacturing Co. Jacobs remained with the company until the 1960s. After the takeover, it was known as the Hertz Drive-Ur-Self System.

The heart logo was used for vehicles manufactured by Hertz in the early 20th century. The shape of the logo came from *'Herz'*, the German word for heart. John Hertz was born Sandor Herz in Ruttka, Hungary. When he was a young boy, his family emigrated to the United States and changed the spelling of their name to reflect how it would be pronounced in German.

The yellow color adopted for the car rental business was an important asset of the brand very early on and can be seen in all the logos that Hertz used over the years. A black-and-yellow variant was used in the late 1940s and early 1950s to emphasize the coast-to-coast coverage Hertz offered.

The famous Hertz logotype with its characteristic unified 'rtz' was introduced in 1963. The logo was restyled in 1982, adding heavy drop shadows, thus expressing strength and portraying Hertz as a major player in the business.

Trying to convey a friendlier image, Hertz introduced a new logo with a softer, cleaner logotype in 2009, accompanied by the slogan 'Journey On'. As the company puts it, the logo expresses "speed, first class service and quality."

Old and new logos together, Basel, Switzerland, 2011

early 20th century

RENT A NEW CAR FROM
HERTZ
and Drive it yourself

1940s

1949

ca 1957

1961

1963, Lippincott & Margulies

1982

2009, Landor Associates

1958 CHEVROLET!

available now
with Turboglide at
HERTZ RENT A CAR
offices everywhere

That's The Hertz Idea! Right now, Hertz has the car you've been waiting to drive. The exciting Chevrolet for 1958!

Just show your driver's license and proper identification at your local Hertz office. You'll get a new Turboglide Chevrolet Bel Air—fully equipped from radio to power steering—at the regular Hertz rate. National average for a '58 Chevy or other fine car is only $7.85 a day plus 9 cents a mile. And that covers *all* gasoline, oil and proper insurance.

Go anywhere! Hertz has over 1,400 offices in more than 900 cities around the world. More offices in more cities *by far* where you can rent, leave and make reservations for a car!

To be sure of a car at your destination—anywhere—use Hertz' fast, efficient reservation service. Call your courteous local Hertz office. We're listed under "Hertz" in *alphabetical* phone books everywhere! Hertz Rent A Car, 218 South Wabash Avenue, Chicago 4, Illinois.

"Rent it here . . . Leave it there" Now, nation-wide at no extra charge!

(Between Hertz cities on rentals of $25 or more. For Chevrolet sedans and comparable models only.)

More people by far... use
HERTZ
Rent a car

'1958 Chevrolet!', ad, USA, 1957
Opposite: 'You can rent a new car from Hertz and drive it yourself...', ad, USA, 1947

You can Rent a New Car From Hertz

and drive it yourself...

...available coast to coast and in Canada

Yes, from coast to coast and in Canada, the long established Hertz system makes it possible to rent big new Chevrolets and other fine cars, completely serviced and properly insured, and drive them yourself! Millions of people do it regularly . . . pleasure seekers, traveling men, many businesses. They save time, banish worries, save money. Hertz, remember, is the only rent-a-car system operating coast to coast and in Canada, trustworthy, uniform, and quickly available in the 250 cities where you'll see the Hertz black and yellow sign. It's so easy to arrange, and costs less than you'd think.

If you are planning a trip, you can now make complete arrangements for car reservations at your destination before you leave home through the new PLANE-AUTO and the RAIL-AUTO TRAVEL PLANS. Consult your local plane or train ticket seller for full particulars.

Call your local Hertz station listed in the telephone classified section for complete information about the Hertz easy rental plan. For FREE Directory of *all* Hertz stations throughout United States and Canada—write Hertz Drivurself System, Dept. 1117, Pontiac, Michigan.

Important Announcement

The Hertz Drivurself System has under way a plan of expansion to serve more cities and towns. Licenses are being awarded to qualified local interests to operate in the Hertz system, the world's largest drivurself organization. Write Hertz Drivurself System, Dept. 1117, Pontiac, Michigan, for complete information about this unusual profit opportunity.

Rent a new Car from HERTZ as easy as ABC

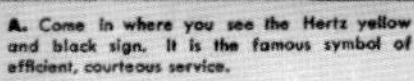

A. Come in where you see the Hertz yellow and black sign. It is the famous symbol of efficient, courteous service.

B. Show your driver's license to the attendant. You will find him always happy to serve you and serve you well.

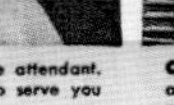

C. Drive away in a Chevrolet, or other fine car, as private as your own, beautifully conditioned, properly insured.

This is the sign of America's only nation-wide Drivurself system.

44 HOLIDAY INN

1952, Memphis, TN, USA
Founder **Kemmons Wilson** Company **Holiday Inn Hotels** HQ **Atlanta, GA, USA**
www.hertz.com

Holiday Inn with the 'Great Sign', USA, ca 1960

Kemmons Wilson's love of travel and the disappointing quality of roadside motels during a family road trip to Washington DC in the summer of 1951 inspired his involvement in the development of Holiday Inn. The new concept promised reasonably priced accommodations, good service, a clean bed, TV, and air conditioning, with the slogan 'Your Host From Coast to Coast'.

Architect Eddie Bluestein came up with the name Holiday Inn as a joke, refering to the 1942 musical film starring Bing Crosby. The first Holiday Inn opened on Summer Avenue in Memphis, the main highway to Nashville, in 1952. The characteristic reverse italic script became the first logo, accompanied by the 'Great Sign'. The standard version in bright green, orange and yellow, Wilson's mother's favorite colors, stood five stories tall and sixteen feet wide. By 1970, it had become an unmissable iconic feature at 1200 Holiday Inns worldwide.

Around 1980, when Wilson left the company, the 'Great Sign' was phased out of the picture. A stylized radiant star, taken from the peak of the 'Great Sign', was added to an updated logotype.

The Intercontinental Hotels Group, which currently owns the Holiday Inn brand, completely modernized the entire hotel chain in 2007. The relaunch included a new logo in vibrant greens, featuring a large 'H' and adding a more business-like style.

Holiday Inn®

1952, James A. Anderson Sr. *('Great Sign')*

ca 1980

2007, Interbrand

45 HP

1939, Palo Alto, CA, USA
Founders **Bill Hewlett, David Packard**
Company **Hewlett-Packard Company**
HQ **Palo Alto, CA, USA**
www.hp.com

Bill Hewlett and Dave Packard founded the technology company in 1939 in a small garage. It is said that they decided on the order of the names with a coin toss.

The 'hp' customized lowercase initials encased within a circle appeared in 1941. The logo was simplified in 1946 to improve legibility and make it easier to engrave on products. That basic form would stand for over 20 years.

HP's physical expansion paralleled the company's product diversification. In 1967, shortly after the introduction of the first HP computer, the logo was restyled to look more contemporary. However, this logo did not fit most products very well, and a modified logo was developed for that specific purpose.

The next iteration of the logo adapted the shape of the logo to conform to the products. The stacked company name used a unique typeface, known as HP Gothic.

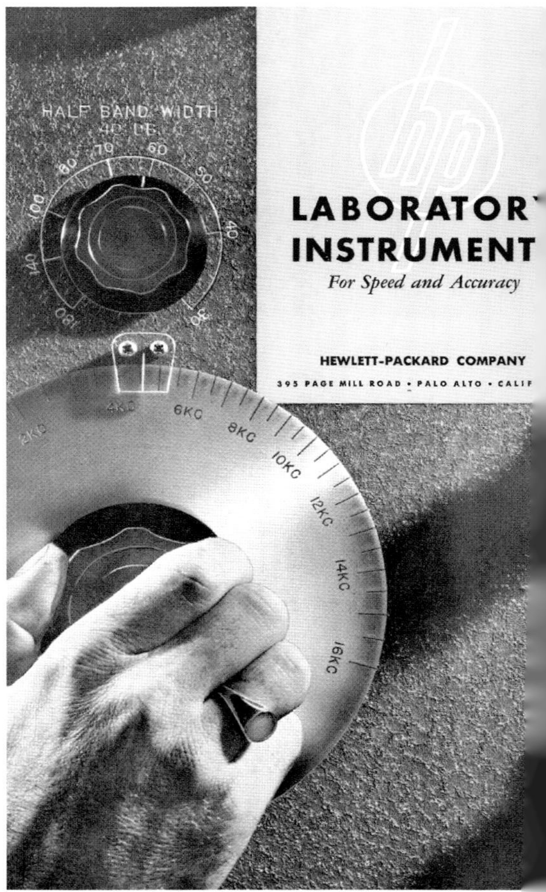

HALF BAND WIDTH
LABORATOR
INSTRUMENT
For Speed and Accuracy
HEWLETT-PACKARD COMPANY
395 PAGE MILL ROAD • PALO ALTO • CALIF

Packaging for printer cartridge, 2009
Top right: 'Laboratory instruments for speed and accuracy', product catalog, 1943

In 1999, Hewlett-Packard split up in two companies. The computer and imaging divisions retained the HP name, while the measurement instruments and equipment divisions were spun off to form Agilent Technologies. From that point on, the logo no longer contained the full company name. The tagline 'invent' was added, capturing a core value of invention through innovation.

The latest version brings HP back to the circle, masking the two initials. It follows the trend of turning logos into 'shiny buttons', but there is also a 2D solid-color version for corporate documents.

HEWLETT-PACKARD CO.

1939

1941

1946

1967

1968 *(for products only)*

1979

1999, Landor Associates

2008, Liquid Agency

46 IBM

1911, Endicott, NY, USA
Founder **Charles R. Flint** Company **International Business Machines** HQ **Armonk, NY, USA**
www.ibm.com

Now a leading computer technology company, IBM was founded in 1911 when Charles Ranlett Flint merged three companies (Tabulating Machine Company, International Time Recording Company, and Computing Scale Corporation) into the Computing Tabulating Recording Corporation. The company produced a large variety of products, from mechanical time recorders to punchcard systems. Its first logo depicted the company's initials: CTR Co.

In 1924, the company changed its name to International Business Machines Corporation, a more accurate description of the company's focus. Its international ambitions were clearly symbolized by the contemporary sans serif lettering forming a globe.

Shifting its focus from the punchcard tabulating business to computers, the company gave its logo a total makeover in 1947. The full name was abbreviated to IBM and the globe shape was replaced by the Beton Bold font, giving the logo a clear, strong and reassuring look. Several variations were used, from outline to solid, as well as boxed-in versions.

In 1956, when Tom Watson Jr. took position as the new CEO after his father died, he personally hired Paul Rand to redesign the logo. Paul Rand gave the logo a more solid and balanced look by using the City Medium font with its prominent slab serifs.

The classic eight-bar logo for the 'Big Blue', as the company came to be nicknamed, was introduced in 1972, again designed by Paul Rand. The horizontal lines suggested dynamism, speed and innovation.

Rand has said he made this version simply because stripes get noticed, not to suggest scan lines on a monitor, as many people seemed to think. The stripes proved to be a perfect brand asset; IBM successfully used them in a wide variety of publications and advertising materials.

'Electrifying Difference', ad, USA, 1953
Next pages: The famous 'Eye, Bee, M' poster by Paul Rand, 1981

1888 *(International Time Recording Company)*

1891 *(Computing Scale Corporation)*

1911 *(Computing Tabulating Recording Corp.)*

1924

1947

1956, Paul Rand

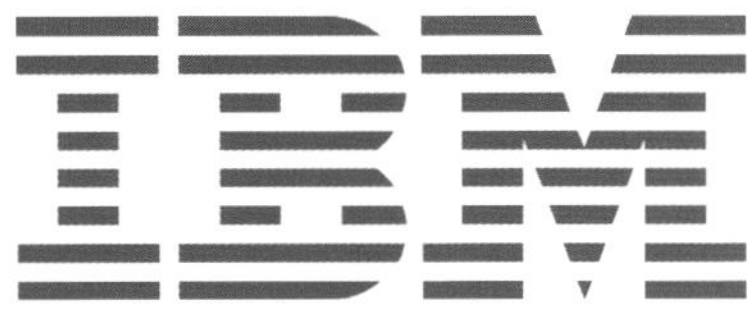

1972, Paul Rand

47 INTEL

1968, Mountain View, CA, USA
Founders **Gordon Moore, Robert Noyce** Company **Intel Corporation** HQ **Santa Clara, CA, USA**
www.intel.com

After using NM Electronics as their first company name for almost a year, Noyce and Moore decided to call their company Integrated Electronics, or Intel for short. The fact that 'intel' is also short for 'intelligence' was a happy coincidence. Noyce and Moore came up with the first logo themselves, with the intriguing dropped 'e'.

Announcing a new era of integrated electronics

A micro-programmable computer on a chip!

intel delivers.

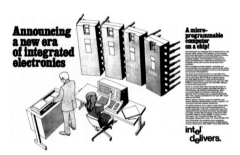

Besides its corporate logo, the script-style 'Intel Inside' logo appeared in ads and on PCs worldwide in 1991, as Intel launched a brand marketing campaign to help users to identify PCs based on Intel microprocessors.

The restyled 2003 Intel Inside logo brought in the dropped 'e' of the corporate logo and moved away from script lettering, while retaining the marker-style circle around it.

In 2006, Intel unveiled a new branding and marketing strategy, including a new logo which would replace both corporate and Intel Inside logos. The advertising tagline 'Leap ahead' was added to communicate "what Intel makes possible in technology, education, social responsibility, manufacturing and more."

Above: 'Announcing a new era of integrated electronics', ad, USA, 1968
Right: Intel Core i7-920 microprocessor, 2008

1969, Robert Noyce & Gordon Moore

1991

2003

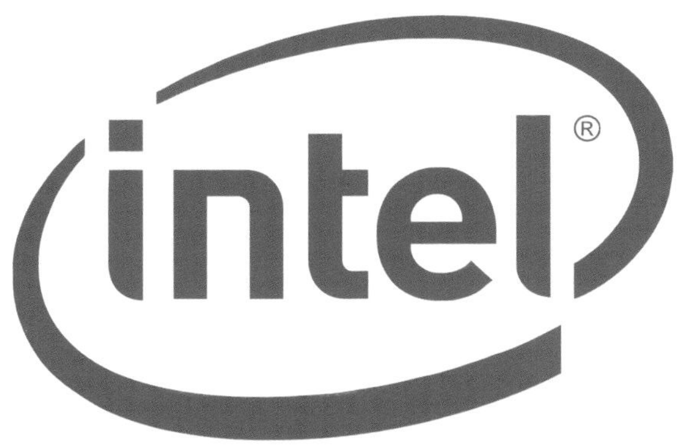

2005, Future Brand

48 JAL

1951, Tokyo, Japan
Founder **Government of Japan** Company **Japan Airlines** HQ **Tokyo, Japan**
www.jal.com

Japan Air Lines Co., Ltd. was established in 1951. The government of Japan recognized the great need for a reliable air transportation system to help Japan grow in the aftermath of World War II. The original logo consisted of the letters 'JAL' stretched out to form wings, captured in an outlined circle.

In 1960, when the airliner entered the jet age, the *'tsurumaru'* logo was revealed, featuring the red-crowned crane. The circle formed by the outstretched wings echoes the national flag. In Japanese culture, the crane is considered a symbol of long life, prosperity and good health. Besides being the national color of Japan, red also represents happiness. The crane symbol would serve the company for the next four decades.

After Japan Airlines was privatized in 1987, the company changed its corporate structure in response to increasing competition. The marketing strategy included a new corporate identity, in which the acronym 'JAL' was displayed prominently on the fuselage of the aircraft. The red square had a fixed position, while the gray bar could be adapted to any length depending on placement. The *tsurumaru* was still shown on the tail, but with the new lettering.

In 2001, after Japan Airlines and Japan Air System merged, a new brand identity was created, which included the 'Arc of the Sun' logo. According to JAL, "the arc that ascends towards the sky symbolizes the sun and stands for joy and exhilaration of customers and the feeling of reaching towards the sky."

From economically tumultuous times, the airline sought a fresh start by returning to the crane logo as a reassuring reminder of the company's happier days. Despite the similarity between the old and new crane, JAL president Masaru Onishi said that JAL is not aiming for a "reconstruction of the past" but a "rebirth".

JAL president Mr. Masaru Onishi and crew in front of Boeing 767-300ER introducing new crane livery, 2011 (Japan Airlines)

1951

1959

1990, Landor Associates

2001, Landor Associates

2011

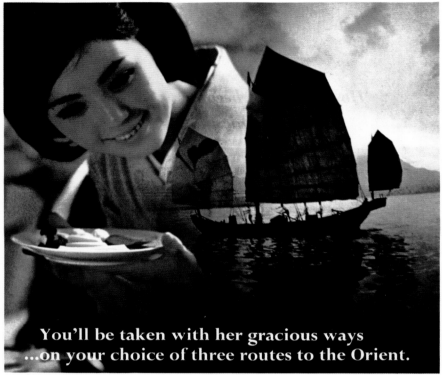

You'll be taken with her gracious ways ...on your choice of three routes to the Orient.

Service is an art
on JAL daily over the Pole,
through the USA,
or east to the Orient.

Step aboard a Japan Air Lines Jet Courier and you enter an atmosphere serene as only the Japanese can make it. You'll find enchanting Japan is with you on all three JAL routes to the Orient.

There's daily service over the Pole, the fastest way to the Orient. Or you can fly transatlantic to the USA and then to Japan. Or follow the historic "Silk Road" through the Middle East and Southeast Asia, to Hong Kong and on to Tokyo.

Whichever way you decide, your comfort aloft is enhanced by the grace and charm of your JAL hostess. She knows only one way to treat you. Like a visitor in her own home.

On JAL you're more than a passenger. You're an honoured guest.

Polar and "Silk Road" flights in cooperation with Air France, Alitalia, Lufthansa.

'You'll be taken with her gracious ways', ad, USA, 1969
Opposite (left to right, top to bottom): JAL timetables for 1953, 1955, 1958, 1961, 1967, and 1976
Note the prototype crane on the 1958 timetable

JAL
JA6002
JAPAN AIR LINES CO., LTD.

EFFECTIVE NOVEMBER 15, 1955
JAPAN AIR LINES
JAL
WINGS OF THE NEW JAPAN
Fly to JAPAN and HONG KONG
from San Francisco and Honolulu via the route of personal service
DC-6B
"Pacific Courier"
TIME TABLES AND FARES

TIME TABLES AND FARES
Effective May 8, 1958
JAL
JAPAN AIR LINES
ROUTE OF THE SUPER COURIER
SAN FRANCISCO
HONOLULU
JAPAN
OKINAWA
HONG KONG
BANGKOK
SINGAPORE

JAPAN AIR LINES
JAL
EFFECTIVE December 1, 1961
— March 31, 1962

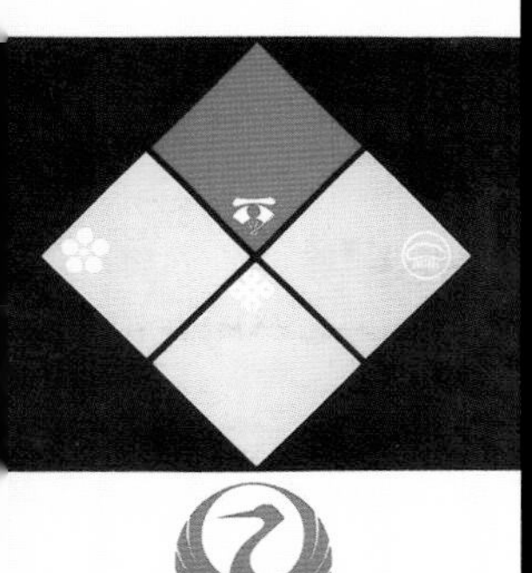

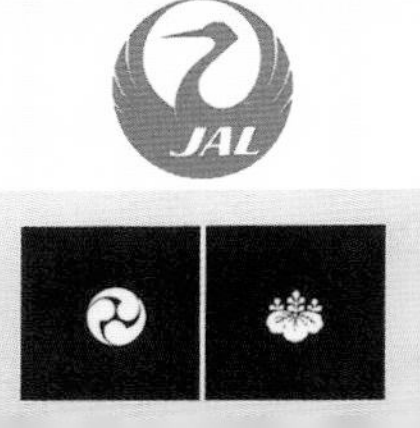
JAL

TIMETABLES · FARES · RATES
JAL
1 EFFECTIVE: MARCH 1 (1967)
JAL
Now JAL can fly you across the Atlantic.
Enjoy gracious JAL hospitality full-circle around the globe.

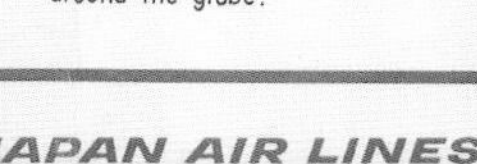
JAPAN AIR LINES

JAPAN AIR LINES
JAL
the worldwide airline of Japan

49 JOHN DEERE

1837, Grand Detour, Ill, USA
Founder **John Deere** Company **Deere & Company** HQ **Moline, Ill, USA**
www.deere.com

The leading manufacturer of agricultural equipment in the world was founded by John Deere in 1837, whose first successes were cast-steel plows. After relocating the company to Moline, Illinois in 1848, John Deere's son Charles boosted nationwide sales through marketing and dealerships in 1869. The first known registered trademark dates back to this period, depicting a running deer jumping over a tree log. As was often the case in these times, the place of manufacture featured prominently in the logo.

In 1912, Deere & Company president William Butterworth, who had replaced Charles Deere after his death in 1907, began the company's expansion into the tractor business and introduced a new logo with a more defined North American white-tailed deer. The original animal had appeared to be a species of deer that is indigenous to Africa. A tagline was also added: 'The trade mark of quality made famous by good implements'.

Top right: Brochure cover, 2011
Below: John Deere road sign, USA, 1966

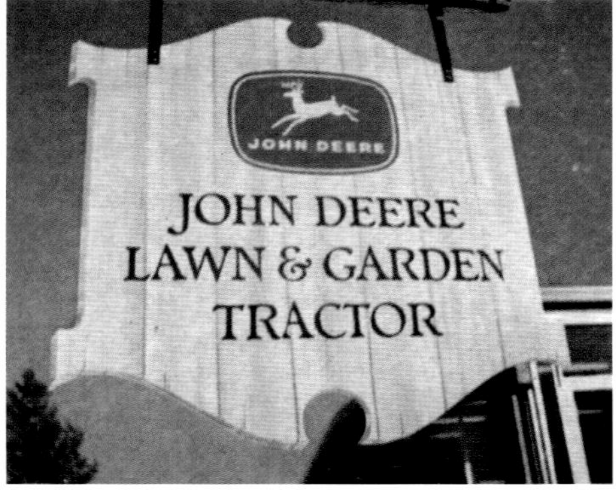

Over the next decades, the logo was gradually simplified. Logo placement on products and other factors led to small, clear changes. 'Quality Farm Equipment' replaced the place of manufacture in 1950, but was dropped again just a few years later.

The deer steadily grew more important, stronger and prouder. All details in the deer and the tree log disappeared, the antlers were turned forward, and four legs became two. The result was a clear, contemporary logo in 1968. A company memo noted, "The new trademark is in keeping with the progress being made throughout all divisions of the company."

In 2000, the dynamic and more muscular-looked stylized deer started to leap forward instead of landing on its front legs. This new pose gave it more elegance and strength.

1876

1912

1936

1937

1950

1956

1968, John Dreyfuss

2000, Landor Associates

50 KFC

1930, North Corbin, KY, USA
Founder **Harland Sanders**
Parent **YUM! Brands** HQ **Louisville, KY, USA**
www.kfc.com

1950s KFC bucket, USA, 2010

Harland 'Colonel' Sanders started his Sanders' Court & Café in 1930, but the chain of fastfood restaurants Kentucky Fried Chicken was founded in 1952. Armed with his classic bowtie, glasses and goatee, the colonel has been part of the logo from the start. Initially serious-looking, he adopted an increasingly bigger smile over the years.

Two years before the colonel's death in 1980, a new logo was introduced. It included smoother features for the colonel and a stacked typewriter-style logotype with an interesting 'K', combining with the dot on the 'i'.

The Kentucky Fried Chicken brand was changed to the abbreviation KFC in 1991 to move away from the somewhat negative connotation of the word 'fried'. In addition, a powerful red was introduced, in combination with a contemporary striping, while keeping the colonel virtually untouched.

When KFC was bought by Tricon in 1997, a new identity was unveiled. The livelier and more prominent colonel, defined in two-color shades, was given a white suit and placed at an angle against a red background without the speed lines.

KFC changed hands again and was sold to Yum! Brands in 2002. In 2007, the colonel's white suit was traded for a red chef's apron, like the one he actually used when he stepped into the kitchen. The streamlined bold black lines gave the face a well-defined and dynamic appearance. A strong black logotype was positioned centered under the chin.

In addition to the abbreviation KFC, the company also started to use the original appellation of Kentucky Fried Chicken again for its signage, packaging and advertising as part of a corporate re-branding program.

KFC restaurant, Harrisburg, IL, USA, 2008 (J. Griffin)

1952, Lippincot & Margulies

1978, Lippincot & Margulies

1991, Schechter & Luth

1997, Landor Associates

2007, Tesser

51 KLM

1919, The Hague, Netherlands
Founder **Albert Plesman** Parent Company **Air France-KLM** HQ **Amstelveen, Netherlands**
www.klm.com

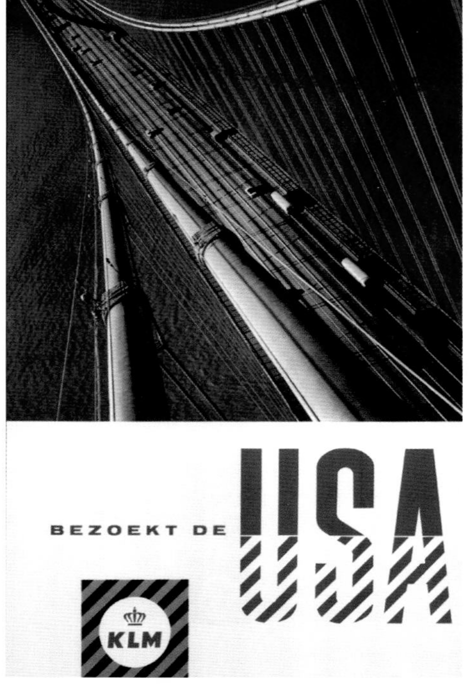

'Visit the USA', poster, Netherlands, 1959

Legend has it that KLM founder Plesman said to his boyhood friend and architect Dirk Roosenburg: "Say Dirk, old boy, can you quickly put together a little vignette for me?" The first logo of the 'Koninklijke Luchtvaart Maatschappij' depicted a crown, since the company had received its royal charter from Queen Wilhelmina. The wings seemed the logical choice for an airline and the interwoven initials are typical for the period. Due to legibility problems, the acronym 'KLM' was placed beside the logo on most official communications.

In the 1930s, the KLM initials appeared as part of the logo, shown in bold italic sans serif caps with an outline drop shadow, but maintaining the winged crown as a hallmark of quality.

Rarely seen in Europe, a different logo in Art Deco style was used on the West Indies routes to and from Miami; the interwoven initials on the shield were even harder to read here. In later iterations, the wings were dropped, but the logo retained the crown symbol.

During the 1950s and 60s, there was no consistent image in terms of color, as several different combinations of reds and blues were used for the logos. 1968 saw a new logo with a crown that was stripped down to the core. Already designed in 1961 by F.H.K. Henrion, it was considered too progressive despite keeping the 'lines' background, much to Henrion's dislike.

Finally convinced, the company removed the lines and circle in 1971, eventually resulting in the single blue KLM logo in 1991 for consistency and easier recognition.

KLM's current livery

1919, Dirk Roosenburg

1930s

1938-1944 *(for West Indies section only)*

1950

1958, Erwin Wasey, Ruthrauff & Ryan

1961, F.H.K. Henrion *(introduced in 1968)*

1971, F.H.K. Henrion

1991, Henrion Ludlow Schmidt

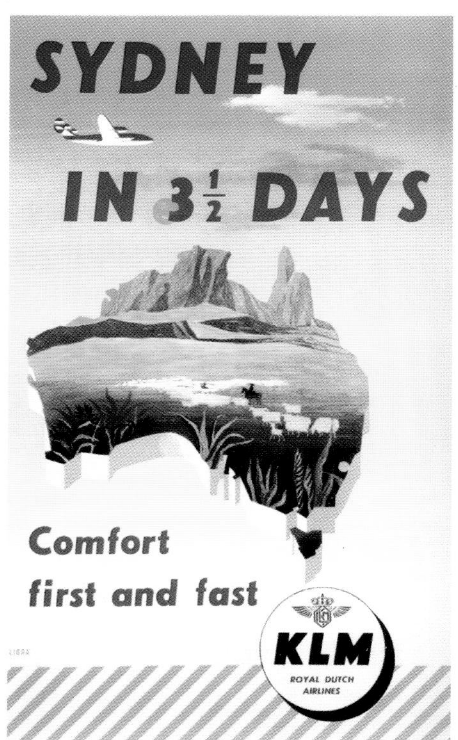

Left: 'Europe in half the time', poster, 1928
Right: 'Sydney in 3½ days', poster, 1950s
Opposite: 'France', poster, 1969

Paris - KLM town par excellence.

france

ROYAL DUTCH AIRLINES

52 KMART

1899, Detroit, MI, USA
Founder **Sebastian S. Kresge** Parent Company **Sears Holding Corporation** HQ **Hoffman Estates, Ill, USA**
www.kmart.com

Kmart signing, 1966

When the first Kmart opened its doors in 1962, just before Walmart was launched later in the year, the S.S. Kresge Corporation already had a long history in discount department stores.

Sebastian S. Kresge, founder of the company, had already invested in 'five and dime' stores in 1897 and owned his first two stores in 1899. In 1929, that number was increased to 597. After turbulent times during the Great Depression, WWII and the rise of the suburbs, the company decided that the new stores would go by the name Kmart. Naturally, the initial K came from Kresge.

The first Kmart logo showed a big, bold, italic red capital 'K' in front of a turquoise lowercase 'mart': a simple but effective approach. The logo would remain largely unchanged until 1990.

In an effort to modernize Kmart and improve its image, the logo was changed in 1990. The angled 'mart' in script lettering is enclosed by an ultra-bold 'K', almost forming a square.

In 2003, going through rough financial times, what was then called the Kmart Holdings Corporation restructured the company and introduced five concept stores with a new logo in a different color scheme: gray and lime green.

In 2004, Kmart purchased Sears, Roebuck and Company and the corporation changed its name to Sears Holdings Corporation.
A redesigned logo showed the full name 'kmart' underlining the big 'K'. This made the logo more flexible, as it was now possible to use the lower case 'kmart' logotype separately as needed. Visit the Kmart website to see an example.

1962

1980 *(Australia)*

1990

2003, Arnell

2004

53 KODAK

1888, Rochester, NY, USA
Founder **George Eastman** Company **Eastman Kodak Company** HQ **Rochester, NY, USA**
www.kodak.com

With the slogan 'you press the button, we do the rest', Kodak's founder George Eastman introduced his photo cameras and photo films in 1888. In the era of glass plates, the easy-to-use cameras and films made photography accessible to everyone.

The word 'Kodak', invented by Eastman himself, was first registered as a trademark in 1888. He explained: "I devised the name myself. The letter 'K' had been a favorite with me. It seems a strong, incisive sort of letter. It became a question of trying out a great number of combinations of letters that made words starting and ending with 'K.' The word 'Kodak' is the result. It is easy to pronounce and spell in any language."

The first logo, a combination of the initials of the company name inside a circle, stood for Eastman Kodak Company, as the company had been called since 1892. Kodak's yellow and red trade colors, introduced in the 1930s and selected by Eastman himself, became one of the company's most valued assets. When Kodachrome film was introduced in 1935, the new logo shifted its focus to the 'Kodak' brand name.

Kodak Petite with EKC logo above the lens ('Charming for any woman. Colors...lavender, blue, gray, green, and old rose. A camera that's almost tiny. Price $7.50, with pouch-type case to match.'), 1930

American advertising from the early 1940s started to show the 'dog-ear' logo, mostly in the lower right corner, suggesting that behind every great picture there is a great brand. Although it would appear in various ways over the years, the 'dog-ear' logo would continue to be used until 1970.

In 1971, the famous yellow box and graphic 'K' element appeared, keeping the slab serif Kodak logotype. This distinctive K element would be Kodak's identifier for the coming 25 years. In the digital age, the big K started to disappear, leaving the logotype, which was updated in 1987, to stand on its own: first by simply taking the existing logotype out of the big K logo, and in 2006 by introducing a new streamlined design.

1907

ca 1935

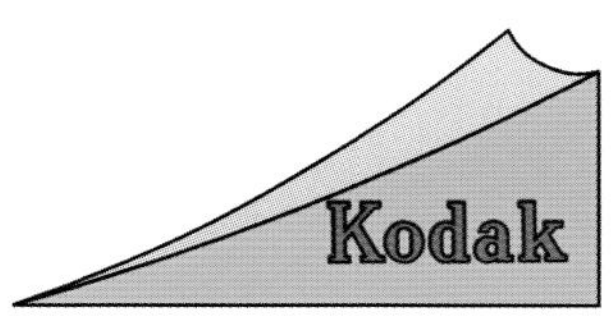

ca 1943

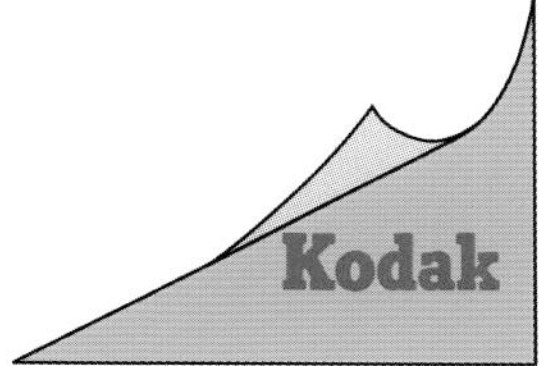

1960s

1971, Peter J Oestreich

1987

1996

2006, Brand Integration Group, Ogily NY

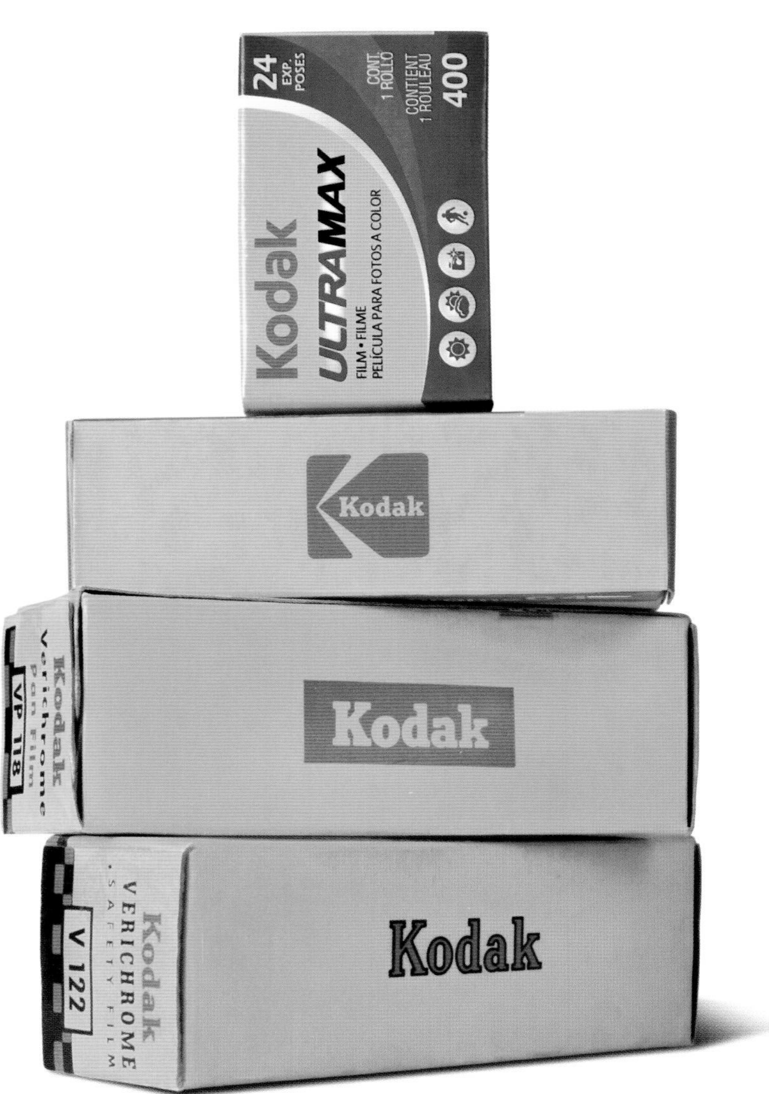

From top to bottom, Kodak Ultra Max (expiry date as seen on box: 2009), Kodachrome 64 (1978), Verichrome Pan (1962) and Verichrome (1956)
Opposite: 'All it does is everything', ad, USA, 1969

INSTAMATIC 133
CAMERA
Kodak
All it does is everything.
The new Kodak Instamatic 133 camera is the one that takes them all—color snaps, black-and-white snaps, and color slides. And when it comes to using the Kodak Instamatic 133 camera, it does just about everything for you. Loading is easy. Just drop in the film cartridge. To shoot, make one simple setting, aim, and press the button. Indoors, just pop on a flashcube and take four flash shots without touching a bulb.
If you don't want to do anything but take good pictures, just see the entire line of new Kodak Instamatic cameras available wherever you see this sign.
Kodak
The Kodak Instamatic® 133 camera.
Kodachrome
TRANSPARENCY
PROCESSED BY
Kodak
Kodachrome
TRANSPARENCY
PROCESSED BY
Kodak
Kodak

54 LEGO

1932, Billund, Denmark
Founder **Ole Kirk Christiansen** Company **Lego Group** HQ **Billund, Denmark**
www.lego.com

Lego block (Lego Group)

The name Lego comes from *'leg godt'* or 'play well' in Danish. The current logo can be traced back to 1953, with the introduction of the cartoon-style white lettering and the black line connecting two dots, symbolizing free spirit and connection. The interlocking building blocks, which had only recently been developed, gave children the freedom to build whatever they wanted.

This early logo is seen in combination with various explanatory terms, such as *'mursten'* (Danish) or *'Bausteine'* (German), both of which translate as 'building blocks'. The term 'System' was also used, and became the definite choice in 1959.

The square was introduced in 1964, giving the brand name more space and a univocal image by acting as an anchor on all packaging and advertising.

By 1973, Lego had dropped the word 'System' from its logo, since the brand was well established. The restyled logo cleverly incorporated the yellow color in a way that made the brand name even more unique and helped it stand out better from the red background.

In 1998, the last restyling shaped the logo as we know it today with slimmer, squared lettering and bolder black outlines for better readability.

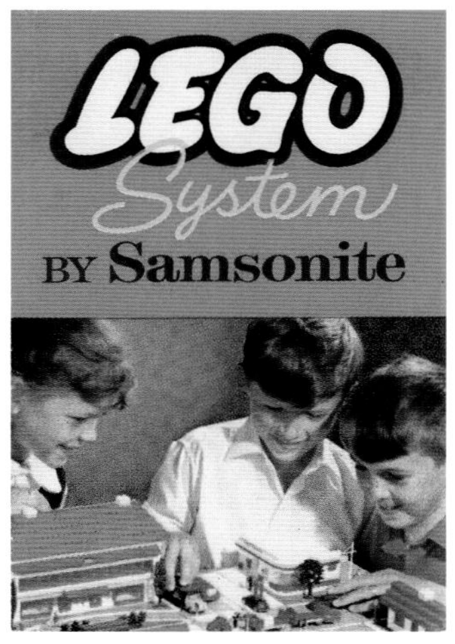

Above: Lego brochure, USA, 1970
Left: Lego box, USA, 1961
(Samsonite manufactured and distributed Lego for the US market from 1961 to 1972)

1934

1936

1936

1946

1950

1953

1954

1955

1959

1964

1973

1998

55 LEVI'S

1850, San Francisco, CA, USA
Founder **Levi Strauss** Company **Levi Strauss & Co**
HQ **San Francisco, CA, USA**
www.levis.com

German-born Levi Strauss was an immigrant to the US in 1847. He established a wholesale dry goods business under his own name, simply Levi Strauss, in San Francisco in 1850, inspired by the California Gold Rush. It was the West Coast branch of his brothers' New York business. After his brother-in-law David Stern became associated with the firm in 1863, the name was changed to Levi Strauss & Co.

Together with Nevada tailor Jacob Davis, he patented the idea of making pants by placing metal rivets at the stress points. The patent was granted in 1873. It was the start of the jeans imperium. Although the company began producing denim overalls in the 1870s, modern jeans were not produced until the 1920s.

The first logo from the 1890s, which is still used on the jeans, depicts a pair of jeans being pulled by two horses going in opposite directions. They are encouraged by two men with whips, putting heavy strain on the material. The picture expressed the heavy-duty quality of the new product.

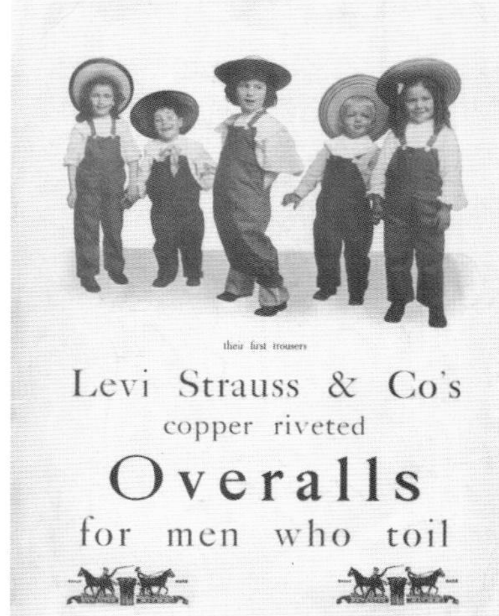

Above: 'Overalls for men who toil', ad, USA, 1905
Right: Red tab label since 1936
Below left: Levi's 501 back label

Several slightly different versions of the illustration were used over the years. As the original logo was a complex picture, a simpler logo was needed for branding purposes. Several logotypes along with the slogan 'America's finest overall' were used prior to the 1940s version, with the characteristic backslanting 'E'. The slogan was changed to 'America's finest overall since 1850'.

In 1969, the distinctive red-and-white 'batwing' was developed to be placed on back pockets. The red shield resembled the pocket's stitch pattern and incorporated the Levi's lettering in a clever mix of uppercase and lowercase letters.

Originally introduced in 1936 to make it easier to recognize a pair of Levi's from a distance, the 'red tab label' became a significant brand element and was used alongside the slightly restyled batwing from 2000 on. A seemingly unbranded version was introduced recently as a logo for Levi's Curve ID product line.

1890s

LEVI'S

1930s

1940s

1969, Landor Associates

2000

2011 *(Levi's Curve ID product line)*

Above: Levi's poster, 1950s
Below: 'I am ready for whatever you throw at me', ad for the Levi's Roadwear campaign by BBH, 2011
Oppostte: 'Miss Levi's', poster by Young & Rubicam, 1970s

LEVI'S

miss Levi's

56 LUCKY STRIKE

1871, Richmond, VA, USA
Founder **R.A. Patterson** Parent Company **British American Tobacco plc** HQ **London, UK**
www.bat.com

'L.S./M.F.T.' ('Lucky Strike Means Fine Tobacco'), ad, USA, 1947

The Lucky Strike brand was introduced in 1871 by the R.A. Patterson Tobacco Company. The name Lucky Strike refered to the Gold Rush. Several types of tobacco products were offered in tins of different sizes with 'R.A. Patterson Tobacco Co. Rich'd Va.' written in the outer circle of the Lucky bulls-eye.

In 1903, Patterson sold Lucky Strike to W.T. Blackwell & Company; two years later, the American Tobacco Company (ATC) acquired the brand. Since 1976, it has been owned by British American Tobacco plc.

In 1917, the Patterson name was removed and the slogan 'It's Toasted' was added.

The production process used for Lucky Strike was unusual, since it included roasting the tobacco. The simplified Lucky Strike logo was shown on the tins. The same logo was used to introduce the cigarettes in the green pack carrying the word 'cigarettes' written in gold letters under the red bulls-eye, progressively growing bigger towards the sides.

Due to the demand for green pigment for the war effort, and an apparent public dislike for the green pack, Raymond Loewy was commissioned to redesign the packaging in 1941. He changed the color green to a fresh and clean white, which he also used for the restyled logo, and put the new bulls-eye on both sides of the pack. This ensured that the logo was always visible, no matter how the pack was placed. The 'Lucky Strike green has gone to war' ad campaign was used to launch the new logo; it was very successful for ATC. The logo is still seen on packs sold today.

Lucky Strike roll cut tobacco tin, ca 1910
Next pages: 'Forever and ever..', ad, USA, 1932

ca 1880

1917

1941, Raymond Loewy

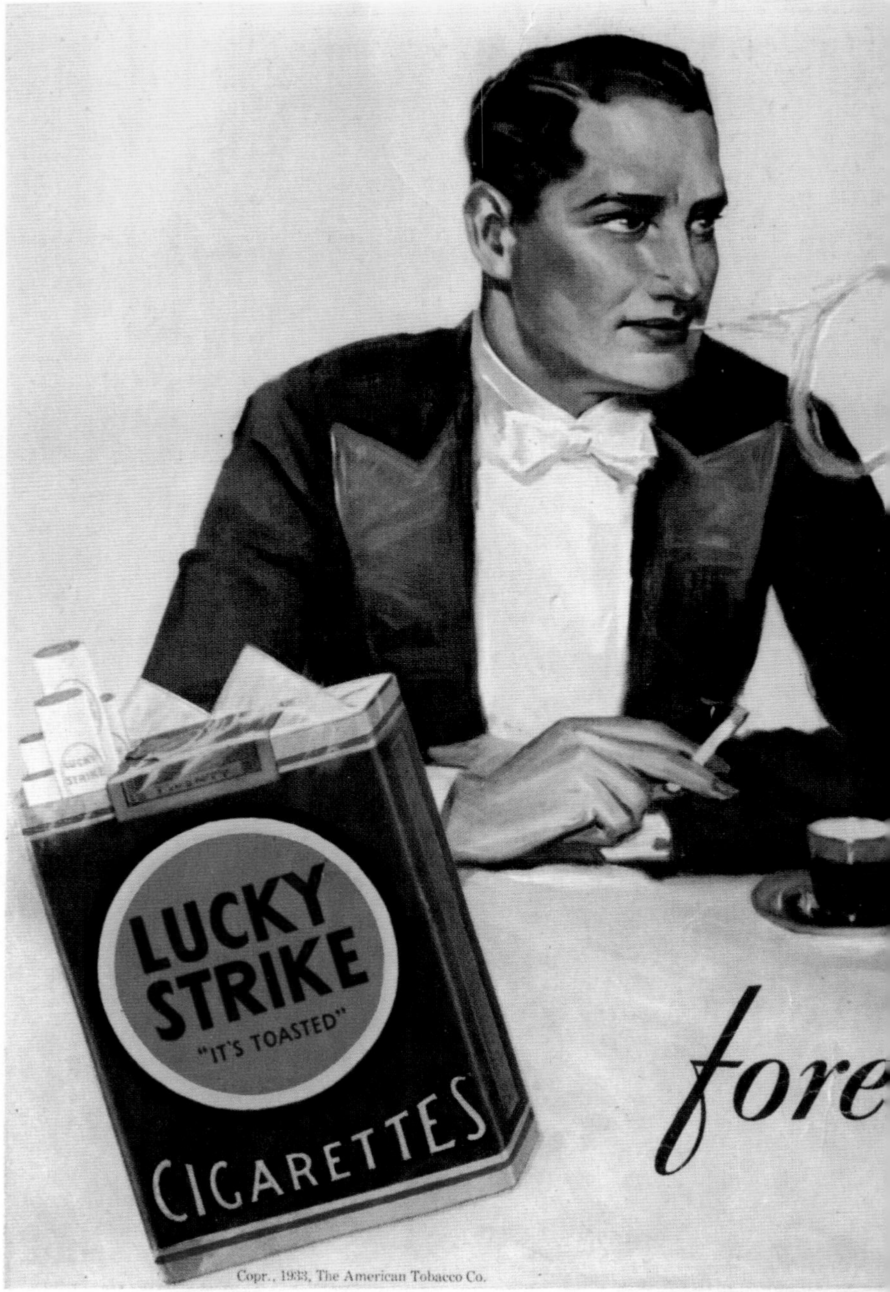
LUCKY STRIKE
"IT'S TOASTED"
CIGARETTES
fore
Copr., 1933, The American Tobacco Co.

Howard Chandler Christy
1932
LUCKY STRIKE
CIGARETTES
LUCKY STRIKE
and ever..

"It's toasted"

57 MASTERCARD

1966, USA
Founders **United California Bank, Wells Fargo, Crocker National Bank, Bank of California**
Company **Mastercard Worldwide** HQ **New York, NY, USA**
www.mastercard.com

In 1966, seventeen bankers formed a federation for the mutual acceptance of their credit cards. Once the federation was formally chartered, the Interbank Card Association (ICA) adopted the 'i' symbol as its logo.

To provide a stronger brand identification, the name was changed into Master Charge. The new logo featured two interlocking circles of red and ocher. The 'i' symbol was retained at the bottom right corner for continuity.

The 'i' symbol was dropped after the name changed from Master Charge to MasterCard in 1979. From this point in time, small changes would be made to keep the logo up to date and to strengthen the brand.

In 1990, a restyled logo was unveiled. It had a new italic lettering and a brighter color scheme. 23 horizontal bars replaced the solid-color area where the two circles interlock.

Because readabilty had suffered slightly after the last change, the number of bars was reduced and a dark blue drop shadow was added to the last logo version in 1996.

Serving a different purpose, the MasterCard Worldwide corporate signature was launched with the announcement that the company was going public in 2006. The logo was created the year before to "complete the transition of MasterCard International from a card payments company to Master Card Worldwide, a leader in advancing commerce globally."

MasterCard logo on ABN Amro credit card, 2011

1966

1967

1979

1990

1996

2005, Future Brand *(corporate logo)*

58 MAZDA

1920, Japan
Founder **Jujiro Matsuda (Mazda Corporation)**
Company **Mazda Motor Corporation**
HQ **Hiroshima, Japan**
www.mazda.com

Mazda's origins can be traced back to Toyo Cork Kogyo Co, which was founded in Hiroshima in 1920. It processed a cork substitute made from the bark of the Abemaki oak tree. When Jujiro Matsuda joined the company in 1927, it shifted to producing tools and vehicles. The Mazda-Go was launched in 1931.

The name Mazda derived from a combination of the god of wisdom, intelligence and harmony, Ahura Mazda, and the founder's name, Jujiro Matsuda. The 1936 winged triple M logo was inspired by the 'Three Mountains' emblem of hometown Hiroshima. It stood for Mazda Motor Manufacturer, and expressed "agility, speed and the ability to soar to new heights."

The production of passenger cars in 1960 marked the beginning of a new era for the company. A completely new identity was introduced, a combination of an encircled 'M' and an all-caps dynamic logotype with distinctive A's.

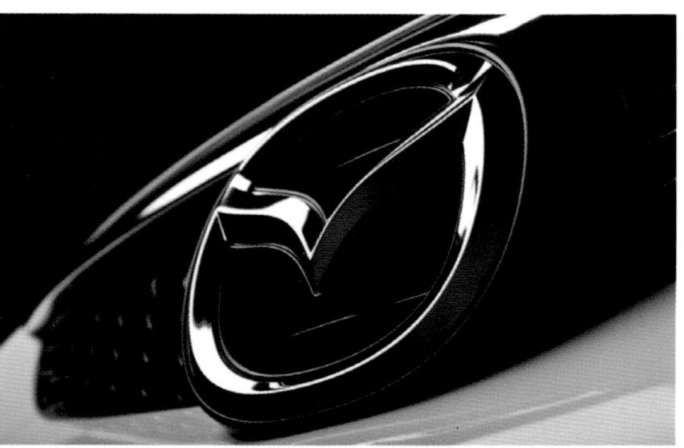

Above: *Mazda's current car badge*
Top right: 'You'll love her for the looks', ad for Mazda 1500, USA, 1969

You'll love her for the looks you'll get.
That's what Mazda 1500 can do for her escort. Because she's suave. And lovely. With graceful curves. And a soft, spacious interior. On the road, she moves like a lady.
Smooth. Quiet. Fast (when
has to be). And always
to your every whim.
Mazda 1500. She has the
to change your world.
make her yours MAZDA
From the world's most progressive automotive plant. Toyo Kogyo Co., Ltd., Hiroshima,

Mazda modernized its logo fifteen years later, along with a completely new corporate identity system, moving to a logotype that is still the basis for the company's identity. From 1991 on, symbols for the export market were added to this logotype. According to Mazda, they represented sun and flame, expressing "heartfelt passion". But the 1991 addition was too similar to Renault's diamond-shaped logo and was altered shortly after.

The most successful logo, known as the 'owl', was introduced in 1997. It depicts stretched wings in flight, and seemingly coincidentally also resembles an 'M'. As Mazda describes it, "The 'V' inside the 'M' spreads out like an opening fan, representing creativity, vitality, flexibility and passion."

1934

1936

1960

1975

1991

1992

1997, Rei Yoshimara

59 McDONALD'S

1940, San Bernardino, CA, USA
Founders **Richard McDonald, Maurice McDonald**
Company **McDonald's Corporation** HQ **Oak Brook, IL, USA**
www.mcdonalds.com

In 1955, Ray Kroc laid the foundation for the world's largest chain of fast food restaurants when he purchased the rights to a small hamburger chain operated by fast food pioneers Richard (Dick) and Maurice (Mac) McDonald.

The brothers called their first restaurant McDonald's Famous Barbecue, which in 1948 changed to McDonald's Famous Hamburgers. Both were typographical logos focusing on the product. The latter depicted a portrait of a chef. The chef evolved into a cartoony character called 'Speedee', when Dick and Mac launched the 'Speedee Service System'. 'Speedee' was a figure with a chef's hat on top of a hamburger-shaped head. It walked quickly and held a sign saying things like 'I'm Speedee', 'Custom built hamburgers', or '15¢'. In a matching style, the McDonald's logotype accompanied Speedee. For signing, a different script logotype was used separately from the mascot.

In 1955, milkshake machine salesman Ray Kroc joined the company as national franchise agent and soon turned McDonald's into the huge company it is today.

Franchise restaurants were built to a standard design, featuring Dick's idea of the Golden Arches. They featured two arches, one on each side of the restaurant, 'holding' the typical slanting roof. After Ray Kroc became full owner of the company in 1961, the arches and roof were the inspiration for the 1962 logo. The idea was to give customers a safe refuge where they could enjoy their break.

In 1968, the logo was changed into the iconic double-arched 'M', now integrating the name McDonald's. In the 1980s, the logo started to appear enclosed in a rounded red rectangle. By then, the company logo had become one of the best-known symbols worldwide. In 2003, McDonald's name was taken from the logo, with the option of still using the logotype separately.

From 2009, the backdrop for the logo changed from red to dark green in Europe. "With this new appearance, we aim to clarify our responsibility for conservation of our natural resources. We will continue to emphasize that priority in future," Hoger Beek, vice chairman of McDonald's Germany, said in the statement.

'Real good...and still only 15¢', ad, USA, 1950s

1940

1948

1953

1962, Jim Schindler

1968

1985

2003

2009 *(Europe)*

Twoallbeefpattiesspecialsaucelettuce-cheesepicklesonionsonasesameseedbun™

You just read the recipe for McDonald's Big Mac™ sandwich.

It starts with beef, of course.

Two lean 100% pure domestic beef patties, including chuck, round and sirloin.

Then there's McDonald's special sauce, the unique blend of mayonnaise, herbs, spices and sweet pickle relish. Next come the fresh lettuce, golden cheese, dill pickles and chopped onion.

And last, but far from least, a freshly toasted, sesame seed bun.

All these good things add up to the one and only taste of a great Big Mac.

Nobody can do it like McDonald's can™

McDonald's®

'Twoallbeefpatties...', ad, USA, 1979

Opposite top: Ray Kroc's first restaurant, Des Plaines, IL, USA, 1955 (McDonald's Corporation)

Opposite below: McDonald's restaurant shaped like a Happy Meal box, Dallas, TX, USA (McDonald's Corporation)

15¢
McDonald's
SPEEDEE SERVICE SYSTEM
HAMBURGERS
OVER 50 MILLION
McDonald's
McDonald's
Drive Thru
MILK SHAKES

60 MERCEDES-BENZ

1926, Stuttgart, Germany
Founders **Karl Benz, Gottlieb Daimler** Company **Daimler AG** HQ **Stuttgart, Germany**
www.mercedes-benz.com

When Gottlieb Daimler and Carl Benz each invented the automobile independently in 1886, the invention revolutionized road transport. Benz founded the firm Benz & Cie. in 1883, and Daimler Motoren Gesellschaft (DMG) was formed in 1890.

They used their own names in the logos. Daimler chose a scripted logotype, while Benz used a cogwheel symbol from 1903, which was replaced with a laurel wreath surrounding the name.

In 1889, Austrian businessman Emil Jellinek began to promote and sell Daimler automobiles. From 1899, he entered race rallies, where he competed under the pseudonym Mercédès, the name of his 10-year-old daughter. Early in 1900, Jellinek made a deal with DMG to sell cars and engines, using Mercedes as the brand name. The Mercedes brand was registered legally in 1902. The all-caps logotype was enclosed in an oval, done simply in black and white.

In 1909, Paul and Adolf Daimler, Gottlieb's two sons, who had become senior executives at DMG, remembered that their father had marked a three-pointed star above his own house on a picture postcard of Cologne and Deutz, and had written to his wife that this star would one day shine over his own factory. It was instantly accepted by the board and both a three-pointed star and a four-pointed

Above: 'Mercedes', poster with 3-pointed star logo above the front grill, ca 1910
Right: 'Mercedes-Benz', poster, 1928

1890

1902

1903

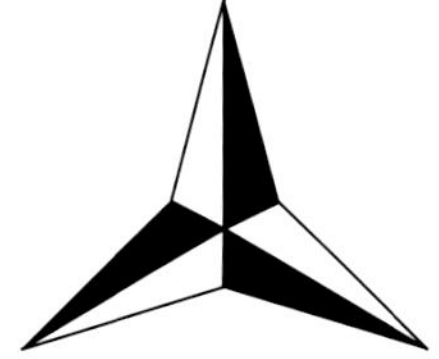

1909, Gottlieb Daimler

1909

1916

1926

1933

1989, Henrion Ludlow Scmidt

2007

2010

star were registered as trademarks; only the three-pointed star was used.

The three-pointed star symbolized Daimler's ambition of universal motorization 'on land, on water and in the air'. Over the years, various small additions were made. In 1916, the star, four small stars and the word Mercedes were integrated in a circle. Alternative versions used the names of the DMG plants at Berlin-Marienfelde or Untertürkheim.

The period of inflation after WWI inspired the former rivals to form a syndicate in 1924 in order to standardize design and production. In 1926, they merged to form Daimler-Benz AG.

A new logo was introduced, combining the main characteristics of both of the previous emblems – the star was surrounded with the brand names Mercedes and Benz, connected by a laurel wreath. Changes to the logo were minimal over the following decades; the iconic three-pointed shape still adorns Mercedes-Benz vehicles and has become synonymous with quality and safety.

Top right: Brochure for 220S/SE, Netherlands, 1959
Below: The already legendary SLS AMG, billboard, UK, 2009

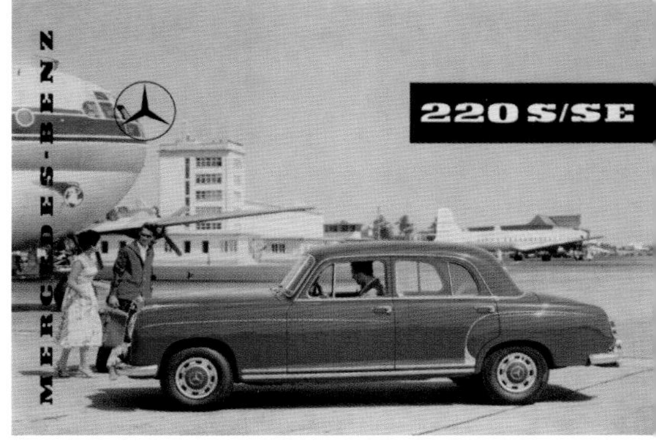

The simpler encircled star, as seen in the famous metal version atop radiator grills from 1921 on, would be used as the Mercedes-Benz logo from 1933 on. Various typefaces would be used for the brand name over the years, but the star remained the same.

In 1989, together with a black and white 3D star with clear ties to Gottlieb's version, a corporate typeface called Corporate A was introduced to maximize brand recognition. After going back to the 'plain' star in 2007, a photographic 3D star was launched three years later, on the eve of the company's 125th anniversary in 2011.

61 MICHELIN

1888, Clermont-Ferrand, France
Founders **Edouard and André Michelin**
Company **Compagnie Générale des Établissements Michelin SCA** HQ **Clermont-Ferrand, France**
www.michelin.com

'Cheers, the Michelin tire will drink up all obstacles!', poster, France, 1898

The Michelin man (Bibendum) mascot was first introduced in 1898 after the founders of the Michelin tire company, brothers Edouard and André Michelin, got the idea from seeing a stack of car tires at the Lyon Universal Exhibition that looked like a human. Artist O'Gallop created the *'Nunc est Bibendum'* poster. *'Bibendum'* in Latin means 'drink up' or 'cheers'; the idea was that Bibendum would drink up all obstacles on the road.

The Bibendum character made the product human, appealing and emotionally accessible. This mascot took on a great number of poses and was used in all media.

His style has changed over the years. Cigar and spectacles disappeared, since they no longer expressed power and success. The many layers of narrow tires have evolved into a smaller number of wider tires, giving Bib a much more contemporary feel. He seems to get slimmer and younger with every generation, making him the friendly and trustworthy icon that he is today.

The first logo from the pre-Bibendium era mentions the cousins Barbier and Daubree who founded the forerunner of Michelin in 1832. Initially producing agricultural equipment, the company shifted to drive belts, conveyors and seals after the invention of vulcanized rubber by Charles Goodyear in 1839.

After the introduction of Bibendum, there was no such thing as a consistent use of logotypes to support Bib. Dozens of different versions were used. Some were combined with a group of Bibendums; from the 1930s on, single figures were often seen.

The 1960s were the start of a more consistent use of logos, with a running Bibendum next to a rolling tire. Around the same time, the Antique Olive logotype finally proved to be a consistent, long-running element for thirty years. The tire was dropped in 1983, leaving a dynamic Bib running even faster and more determined than before.

A new identity was introduced in 1998 in honour of Michelin's 100th anniversary. Besides the modernized logotype, it depicts a strong, athletic Bibendum extending a warm welcome to customers.

ca 1888

Michelin

1898

MICHELIN

ca 1910 *(USA)*

ca 1912 *(UK)*

ca 1914-1920s

1930s

1950

Detail of ad for Michelin ZX radial tires, Netherlands, 1973

ca 1958

1968

1983

(US version with diagonal Michelin bar)

1998

Evolution of Bibendum, 1898-2011

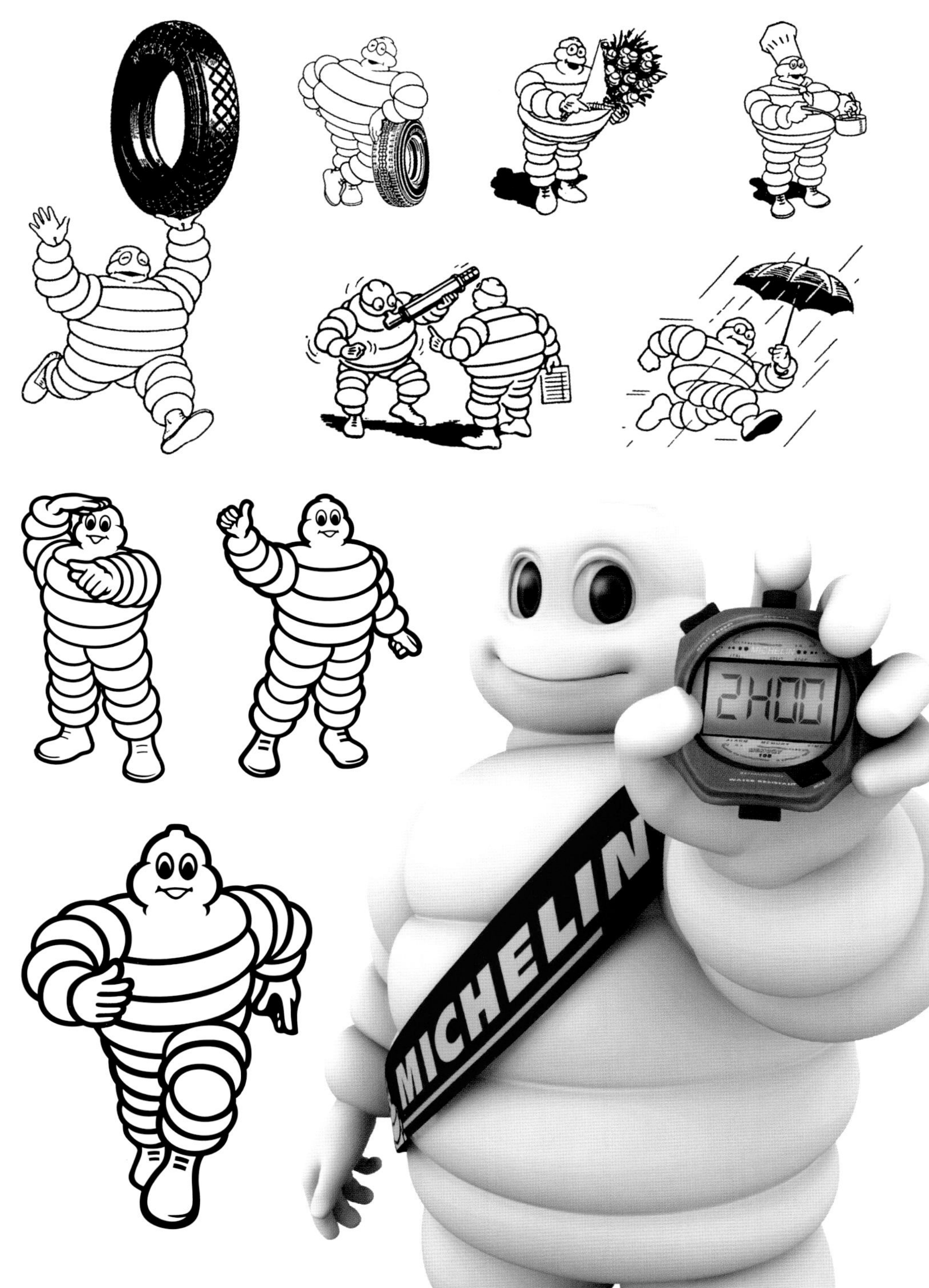
2H00
MICHELI
MICHE

62 MICROSOFT

1975, Albuquerque, NM, USA
Founders **Bill Gates, Paul Allen** Company **Microsoft Corporation** HQ **Redmond, WA, USA**
www.microsoft.com

'Undo. Windows. Mouse. Finally', ad, USA, 1984

In a letter to Paul Allen dated July 29, 1975, Bill Gates used the name 'Micro-Soft' to refer to their partnership. The hyphen in the earliest known written reference never made it to the logo stage.

Symbolizing Microsoft's innovative ideas and advanced computer technology, the first logo shows a fashionable futuristic lettering, each character made up of a series of lines shifting gradually from bold to light, adding a soft touch. In the late 1970s, Microsoft adopted a second logo with sharp-edged lettering that was used for consumer products. The all-caps 'Blibbet' logo, with a central 'O' that referenced the 1976 version in its bold-to-light zooming effect, was introduced in 1982. Beloved by Microsoft employees, when a replacement was proposed in 1987, it was memorialized in a 'Save the Blibbet' campaign by Dave Norris, and honored by the Blibbet Burger served on the Microsoft campus.

In 1987, Microsoft introduced the 'Pacman', based on Helvetica Black Italic. According to Computer Reseller News Magazine, this new Microsoft logo "has a slash between the 'o' and 's' to emphasize the 'soft' part of the name and convey motion and speed."

After 25 years Microsoft unveiled a new logo that was designed by an in-house design team according to the company's own visual language, called Metro. This coherent, clean, typography-led approach was implemented across across its entire portfolio of products. The Segoe font is used for the logotype and on all products and marketing communications. The symbol's colored squares express the company's diverse portfolio of products.

Microsoft store, Oak Brook, IL, USA, 2012 (Michael Kappel)

1976

1978 *(consumer products division)*

1982

1987, Scott Baker

2012, Microsoft

63 MOBIL

1911, New York, NY, USA
Founder **Vacuum Oil** Parent Company **Exxon Mobil** HQ **Irving, TX, USA (Exxon Mobil)**
www.mobil.com

Mobil's roots (and Esso's) can be found in Rockefeller's Standard Oil Trust, which was founded in 1870. Before it fragmented into 33 separate companies in 1911 as a result of the anti-trust ruling by the American Supreme Court, it had grown to be one of the world's largest corporations.

Two companies in that old conglomerate were Vacuum Oil and Standard Oil of New York (Socony). Vacuum Oil already had been selling lubricants using the name Gargoyle Mobiloil, whereas Socony owned the Pegasus brand. When the two companies merged to form Socony-Vacuum Corporation in 1931, the logos also merged into a shield carrying the brand name Mobiloil or Mobilgas and the red flying horse.

In Greek mythology, when Perseus cut off the head of the evil Medusa, a marvellous winged horse emerged from the spot where her blood soaked into the ground. Athena, the Greek goddess of wisdom, named him Pegasus and crafted a golden bridle to tame him. As an enduring symbol of power and speed, Pegasus was a perfect icon for the Socony-Vacuum products.

In 1955, the name was changed to Socony Mobil Oil Company, Inc. Both Mobiloil and Mobilgas logos were replaced by the single brand Mobil. The shield was restyled to accomodate a small Pegasus centered below an emphatic Mobil logotype.

In 1966, the company was renamed the Mobil Oil Corporation, after the company's successful brand. The logotype excelled in simplicity and clarity with the characteristic red 'O'. Tom Geismar, who designed a complete Mobil alphabet, wanted a memorable element in the logo that would help people using the right pronounciation of the brand, stressing the first syllable. The round 'O' recalls the shape of the wheel as the ultimate symbol of mobility, and was also echoed in the architecture of service stations. Pegasus was placed in a white circle, used separately from the logotype.

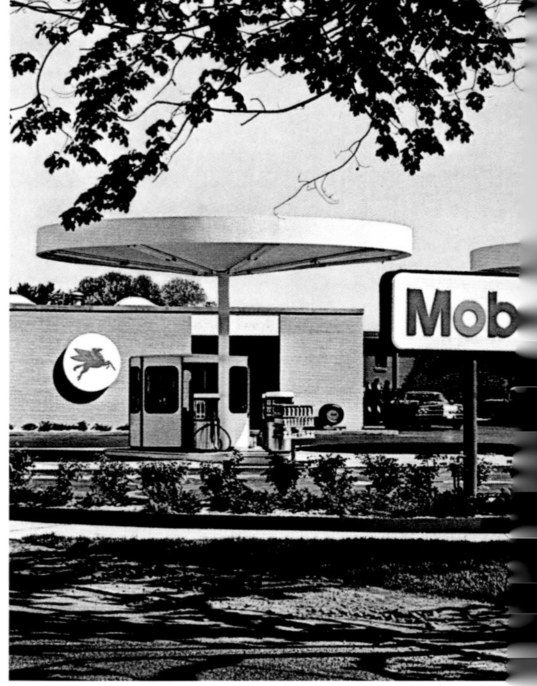

Service station with circular pumps and canopies, USA, 1966

1911

1911

1931

1957

Mobil

1965, Chermayeff & Geismar

Women Drivers

Do they realize the relation of Engine Lubrication to both Petty and Serious Driving Problems?

MORE AND MORE men drivers are realizing the importance of using the correct oil in their cars. To their wives who drive the cars during the week, the importance of scientific lubrication is even greater.

Driving problems, bothersome enough for men drivers, become more serious when a woman is at the wheel.

Among the driving problems which bother women, perhaps the most important are these: 1—Engine is difficult to start. 2—Gears have to be shifted on hills and in traffic. 3—Engine missing because of fouled spark plugs.

Engine difficult to start

Women drivers use cars largely for short trips. Often the car stands idle outside for several hours. While standing it cools off. Starting a cold engine is always more difficult than starting a warm one. But this difficulty of starting is increased by a low quality of wrong-bodied oil which throws an additional strain on the batteries.

The correct grade of Gargoyle Mobiloils often surprises motorists by the easier starting which results. This is because the oil is both of the highest quality and of a scientifically correct body. If the Chart specifies a different grade of oil for your car in winter, be sure to use this grade.

Frequent gear shifting

With incorrect lubrication the engine overheats. The valves become sticky. The spark plugs foul. This results in irregular action of the engine, lessening its power. As a result the engine loses its flexibility to a marked degree. Hills formerly taken on high gear must now be traveled in lower gear. Lower gear has to be used too much in traffic. Trouble of this kind is directly traceable to incorrect lubrication, and can be avoided when the motorist follows the Chart on the right.

Spark plugs foul

Engine missing is quite often caused by a fouled spark plug. Removing and cleaning a spark plug is simple enough to a man, but it is a nasty, troublesome job for a woman. Frequent fouling of spark plugs is usually due to incorrect lubrication. With the correct grade of Gargoyle Mobiloils women drivers will experience a freedom from this kind of trouble.

Other operating troubles frequently encountered are—water boiling in the radiator, due to overheating of the engine; excessive smoking at the exhaust; and other annoyances, all of which are usually traceable to faulty lubrication.

. . . . .

OF ONE THING you may be sure. If you use the grade of Gargoyle Mobiloils specified in the Chart, you are getting maximum freedom from the troubles discussed here. This is a recognized fact in scientific circles and among the more experienced automobile manufacturers, dealers and motorists the world over.

If your car is not listed on the partial Chart to the right send for our booklet "Correct Automobile Lubrication," which contains the complete Chart. Or consult the complete Chart at your dealer's. Be careful to notice what grade of Gargoyle Mobiloils is specified for winter use in your car. In writing, please address our nearest branch.

Mobiloils

A grade for each type of motor

Domestic Branches: New York, Boston, Philadelphia, Pittsburgh, Detroit, Chicago, Minneapolis, Indianapolis, Kansas City, Kan., Des Moines

VACUUM OIL COMPANY *Specialists in the manufacture of high-grade lubricants for every class of machinery. Obtainable everywhere in the world* **NEW YORK, U.S.A.**

Chart of Recommendations for AUTOMOBILES

(Abbreviated Edition)

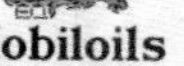

Mobiloils

A grade for each type of motor

How to Read the Chart

THE Correct Grades of Gargoyle Mobiloils for engine lubrication are specified in the Chart below.

A means Gargoyle Mobiloil "A"
B means Gargoyle Mobiloil "B"
E means Gargoyle Mobiloil "E"
Arc means Gargoyle Mobiloil Arctic

These recommendations cover all models of both passenger and commercial vehicles unless otherwise specified.

Where different grades of Gargoyle Mobiloils are recommended for summer and winter use, the winter recommendation should be followed during the entire period when freezing temperatures may be experienced.

This Chart is compiled by the Vacuum Oil Company's Board of Automotive Engineers, and constitutes a scientific guide to Correct Automobile Lubrication.

If your car is not listed in this partial chart, consult the Chart of Recommendations at your dealer's, or send for booklet, "Correct Lubrication," which lists the Correct Grades for *all* cars.

NAMES OF AUTOMOBILES AND MOTOR TRUCKS	[illegible]		[illegible]		[illegible]		[illegible]		[illegible]	
	Summer	Winter	Summer	Winter	Summer	Winter	Summer	Winter	Summer	Winter
[illegible]	[illegible]	[illegible]	[illegible]	[illegible]	[illegible]	[illegible]	[illegible]	[illegible]	[illegible]	[illegible]

Want to see America best? See your Mobil dealer first

A family restaurant or a thrill-filled rodeo. The trained Mobil dealer can help you find either—and aid you in dozens of other ways, too. He's trained to take the guesswork out of travel.

Let Mobil Be Your Travel Guide. Thousands of Mobil dealers attend a special class to help them take the guesswork out of travel. Here's what they can do for you:

1. Be Your One-Man Travel Center

The Mobil dealer can help plan your trip. With the new Mobil Travel Guide, he can give you:

- Accurate, frank 1-to-5-star QUALITY RATINGS on over 20,000 hotels, motels and restaurants—plus facts on prices, service and [illegible] values.
- Latest information on places to visit—[illegible], historical sites, state and national parks all over the country.
- Hard-to-get facts about baby sitters, laundry service, [illegible], picnic spots, swim facilities for children and pets.

[illegible]

[illegible]

The 1965 Mobil Travel Guide comes in 7 completely new regional editions covering 48 states. Copies are on sale for $1.50* at many Mobil dealers.

[illegible] New York City, the Henry Ford Museum in Dearborn, Mich., and on Gray Line Sightseeing Tours.

[illegible] "Rated—1965 Mobil Travel Guide" sign.

2. Local Travel Information

The Mobil dealer knows his area [illegible] ... [illegible] information as well. It's all part of his special training.

Many dealers have for your use an exclusive 128-page Travel Directory, containing up-to-date sources of local travel literature about camping, fishing and vacation activities.

3. Reliable Mobil Maps

The Mobil dealer can provide you with reliable, easy-to-read Mobil maps ... and help plan your trip in advance by ordering specially marked maps showing the best [illegible] route to your destination.

4. Quality Products for your Car

Long vacation miles make your car work extra hard. The Mobil dealer has quality products to keep it running smoothly—including Mobil Premium ... High Energy Gasoline.

5. Charge it with a Mobil Credit Card

Need gasoline, oil, tires, a new battery or a lubrication? With a Mobil Credit Card, you can say "Charge it" to any Mobil dealer from coast to coast. Mobil tires and batteries may be purchased on convenient extended terms.

For good advice ... and good products ... depend on your Mobil dealer

Mobil®

◄Best place in Cheyenne to stay with a family? A Mobil dealer helps Mr. [illegible] of Denver find out in advance.

Mobiloil Again

FIRST AT INDIANAPOLIS

Troy Ruttman —1952 winner of the Indianapolis Speedway Classic, one of the world's toughest auto races—smashed all records by averaging 128.922 m.p.h. for 500 scorching miles! Ruttman used triple-action Mobiloil in his winning car. Why not give your car's engine this same winning protection against wear? Insist on —be sure you get—triple-action Mobiloil!

Mobiloil — World's Largest-Selling Motor Oil!

Why Accept Less For Your Car?

SOCONY-VACUUM OIL COMPANY, INC., and AFFILIATED COMPANIES THROUGHOUT THE WORLD

'First at Indianapolis', ad , USA, 1952
Opposite top: 'Women drivers', ad, USA, 1921
Opposite below: 'Want to see America best', ad, USA, 1965

64 MTV

1981, New York, NY, USA
Founder **Robert Warren Pittman, Warner Communications**
Company **MTV Networks** HQ **New York, NY, USA**
www.mtv.com

"Ladies and gentlemen, rock and roll." On August 1, 1981, these words launched MTV on American television. The initial broadcast started with the original MTV theme song accompanying photos from the Apollo 11 moon landing; the flag showed that first iconic MTV logo in constantly changing colors and designs.

Still from MTV 'Moon' leader, 1981

The first roughs showed a hand holding a tomato portrayed as a music note and the name 'The Music Channel'. This concept was apparently not well received. The first logos played around with just the letters 'MTV', resulting in the famous script 'TV' partly covering the big blocky 'M'.

The MTV identity broke all the rules of what a classic corporate identity should be, with a logo that was constantly changing, just like the music itself. Without altering the basics, the logo would be dressed up in polka dots, stripes, fur, metal or what-have-you in any color and in any style possible. It was a smart way to keep the brand alive and an ongoing inspiration for contributing designers from around the globe.

In 2009, MTV decided to take a new approach. The logo would be used in black on a white background only. The MTV logo remained onscreen at all times in a fixed, top-left position and acted as an anchor for the new, flexible typographic navigation system for displaying onscreen information. As part of this change, various filmmakers were invited to create motion graphics pieces or 'sound sculptures'.

The MTV brand has represented more than 'music television' for many years. By the end of 2009, the words 'music television' were no longer included in the official logo, which is now cropped at the bottom. The new logo can also be used as a see-through window, showing what is happening on MTV at any given time.

Logo for MTV Video Music Awards, 2009

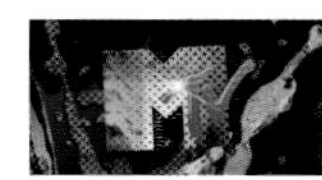

1981, Manhattan Design. 1981-2009, various designers

2009, Popkern

MUSIC TELEVISIO
mobil
hi
performan

MTV sign at MTV Networks Benelux HQ,
Amsterdam, Netherlands, 2011

65 NASA

1958, USA
Founder **Government of the USA** HQ **Washington DC, USA**
www.nasa.gov

The first logo of the National Aeronautics and Space Administration was a seal symbolizing space exploration, scientific discovery and aeronautics research. It depicted two planets in space with stars, an orbital path, the red chevron (a hypersonic wing representing aeronautics) and the agency's full name, all enclosed in a circle. It is still used for formal ceremonies.

The 'meatball' logo was designed by James Modarelli, the head of NASA's Lewis Research Center Reports Division, in 1959. It gave NASA a less formal look than the government insignia, while using only the national red, white and blue. Pared down to the essentials, it focused on the initials, the chevron and the orbital path.

As part of the US Federal Design Improvement Program in the 1970s and in an effort to meet the growing demands of NASA's technological accomplishments, a strikingly simple and futuristic logo, the 'worm', was created in 1974. Not just a logo, it was part of a comprehensive brand identity system, winning a Presidential Award for Design Excellence in 1984.

The 'meatball' logo returned from retirement in 1992. Accounts vary as to why it was brought back; some say it was to recapture the magic after the Challenger space shuttle crashed, while others claim that long-term opponents of the 'worm' had finally triumphed.

Space Shuttle Enterprise flies free of the 747 Shuttle Carrier Aircraft during approach and landing tests, 1977 (NASA)

1958

1959, James Modarelli

1974, Danne & Blackburn

1992, James Modarelli

66 NICKELODEON

1977, New York, NY, USA
Founder **Warner Communications** Company **MTV Networks** HQ **New York, NY, USA**
www.nick.com

Pinball theme ident, 1981

Originally called Pinwheel when it debuted in 1977, children's TV channel Nickelodeon (or 'Nick' for short) was renamed at its relaunch in 1979. Besides the logotype, the first logo included a mime peeking into the 'N', as if it were a Nickelodeon machine. The mime performed in between programs as a filler, turning the crank on the machine as soon as the next program was about to start. Difficult to implement in smaller sizes, the logo was replaced in 1980 and the descriptor 'The Young People's Channel' was added.

In 1981, a colorful logotype was introduced that was all capitals except for the 'i', which resembled a stylized outline of a child. A pinball theme was used for the network's TV idents.

The 1984 identity, created with the trademark properties 'flexible', 'irreverent' and 'bright color' in mind, used Balloon Extra Bold for the basic logotype. Nickelodeon's brand promise - 'Kids first' - was visualized by the playful use of a large number of background shapes, supporting Nickelodeon's diverse programming and various business lines.

Celebrating its 30th anniversary in 2009, a new identity was announced to unify Nickelodeon with its four sister channels: Nick at Nite, Nicktoons, Noggin, and The N. Along with the new logo, The N was rebranded as TeenNick and Noggin as Nick Jr., bringing the orange 'Nick' into all of its channels. *Variety* reported: "The decision to streamline the network identities came after they started putting all of the channels' logos on the same business card and decided that it looked like a mess." As in 1981, the focal point of the logo is the letter 'i', the two parts now melted into one, underlining the resemblance to the stylized outline of a child.

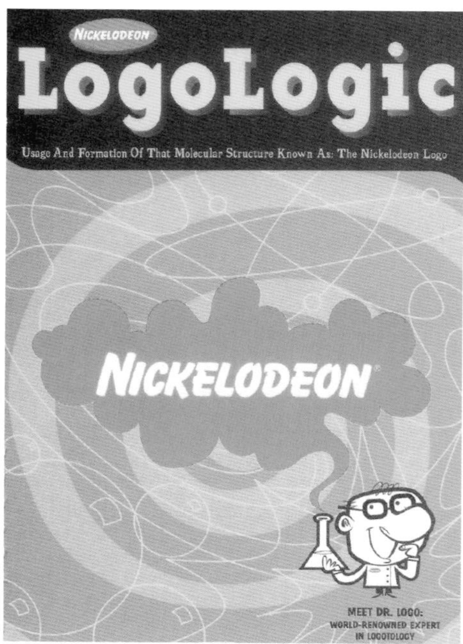

Cover of Nickelodeon's 'Logo Logic' manual, 1998

Nickelodeon

Nickelodeon

1979

1980

NICKELODEON

1981, Lou Dorfsman

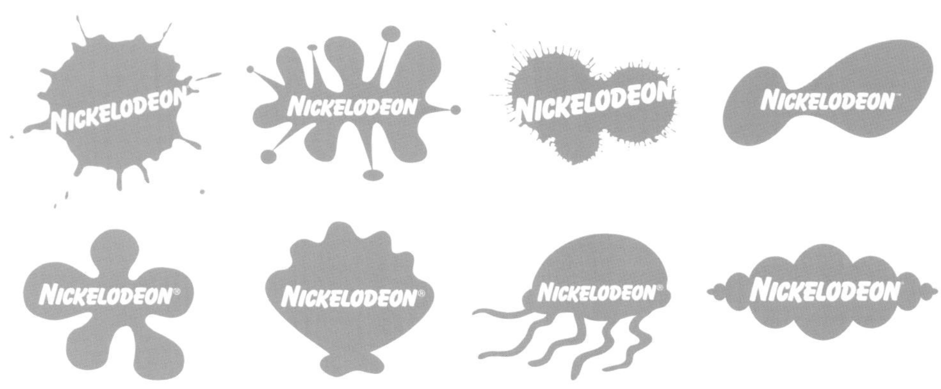

1984, Scott Nash and Tom Corey

nickelodeon

nick jr. teennick

nicktoons nick@nite

2009, Eric Zim

67 NIKE

1964, Portland, OR, USA
Founders **Bill Bowerman, Philip Knight** Company **Nike Inc.** HQ **Beaverton, OR, USA**
www.nike.com

Nike ad from the 'just do it' campaign, 1980s

The sportswear and equipment company was founded in 1964 by Bill Bowerman and Philip Knight as Blue Ribbon Sports. Initially distributing the Japanese Onitsuka Tiger shoes, the Nike brand was introduced in 1971, when BRS launched their own line of sports footwear. The name Nike is taken from the Greek goddess of victory, expressing ambition and a strong will to win.

Portland State University graphic design student Carolyn Davidson created the famous 'Swoosh' logo. Inspired by the winged goddess, it suggested movement and speed. After rejecting various other designs and under pressure to meet production deadlines, Philip Knight chose the swoosh, saying: "I don't love it, but it will grow on me."

Davidson only charged the company $35 for the design. However, after working for Nike for several more years, she was given a diamond Swoosh ring and an undisclosed number of Nike stocks when she left the company in 1983.

In 1978, when the company became Nike, Inc., the logo was changed. The swoosh was placed at a different angle to embrace the new, all-caps logotype. The 'Swoosh' became synonymous with the company. The symbol and the 'just do it' slogan captured the essence of the brand.

After 25 years of use, the iconic 'Swoosh' was instantly recognized. Starting in 1995, the brand name was removed from the logo.

1971, Carolyn Davidson

1978, Nike

1985, Nike

1995, Nike

68 NIKON

1917, Tokyo, Japan
Founders **3 leading optical manufacturers**
Company **Nikon Corporation** HQ **Tokyo, Japan**
www.nikon.com

Nikon was founded in 1917 as Nippon Kogaku Kogyo Kabushikigaisga (Japan Optical Industries Corporation), also abbreviated to Nikko, from a merger of three leading Japanese optical glass manufacturers. With the end of WWII, production shifted to cameras, microscopes, binoculars, surveying instruments, measuring instruments and ophthalmic lenses.

In 1946, the Nikon brand name was adopted for small-sized cameras. When Nikon Inc. was established in 1953, the logo changed to achieve a more international look. The *New York Times* raved about the Nikon's superior quality, which boosted sales in the US. The logotype would change several times during the 1950s and 60s, eventually evolving into the famous 'pill' logo in 1965.

When the company was renamed Nikon Corporation in 1988, the logo was restyled. The oval 'pill' shape was replaced by a yellow rectangle with blue bars either above and below or to the left and right of the Nikon 'brick'.

Around 1998, the assortment of various blocks was reduced to just one clean, strong yellow square. The logotype remained unchanged.

Seeking solutions to visualize concepts for 'innovative technology' and 'sense of the times', a sequence of rays was added in the 2003 version of the logo. According to the press release, the sequential rays "represent the future, and express Nikon's mission, will and future possibilities."

Top: Nikon SP, brochure, 1960s. Right: Nikon FM, poster, 1970s

1920s

ca 1930

1940s

ca 1953

Nikon

1950s

ca 1960

ca 1965

1988

ca 1998

2003, Interbrand

69 NIVEA

1911, Hamburg, Germany
Founders **Paul C. Beiersdorf (Beiersdorf), Dr. Oscar Troplowitz (Nivea)**
Company **Beiersdorf AG** HQ **Hamburg, Germany**
www.beiersdorf.com, www.nivea.com

German skin and beauty care company Beiersdorf was founded by pharmacist Paul C. Beiersdorf in 1882, when he was granted a patent to manufacture medical plasters. The company was acquired in 1890 by another pharmacist, Dr. Oscar Troplowitz, who continued operating under the Beiersdorf name, which was already well known.

Dr. Isaac Lifschütz, who would join Beiersdorf later, applied for a patent for the emulsifying agent Eucerit in 1900. Made from lanolin, it was the basis for Eucerin and was also used for Nivea starting in 1911. The name of this new product came from the Latin word *'niveus'* (white as snow). The invention of a stable water-in-oil creme marks the birth of what is now the world's largest body care brand.

The first Nivea creme was sold in a yellow tin with red and green graphics in Art Nouveau style. A similar style and color scheme were used for the 1924 restyling.

Blue and white became the primary brand colors in 1925. The Nivea logo was modernized and set in an all-capital serif font. Placed in white on a blue background, the tin became a timeless design classic.

In the 1930s, the characteristic blue-and-white color scheme of the packaging range for this rapidly expanding range of skin care products was seen not only in print ads and point-of-sale materials, but also in early film advertising. The Art Deco Futura-esque logo appeared in 1935, and would see only minor changes until the advent of the 1970 version which is still in use today.

First and current Nivea Creme tin, 1911 and 2007 (Beiersdorf)

Nivea celebrated its 100th birthday in 2011. Although the Nivea brand hosts a vast range of skin care products, the creme tin is still the most popular product. It is now represented in the general Nivea brand logo, which is a blue circle with the famous logo in white in the centre.

Nivea

1911

Nivea

1924

NIVEA

1925

NIVEA

1931

NIVEA

1935

NIVEA

1949

1970

2011

Nivea-

Creme ⋆ Puder

Seife

Left: 'The crème de la crème', ad, Germany, 1971
Right: 'For skin protection', ad, Austria, 1950s
Below: 'Nivea cream protects against sunburn', ad, Germany 1928
Opposite: 'Nivea cream, powder, soap', ad, Germany, 1924
(all ads: Beiersdorf)

70 NOKIA

1865, Tampere, Finland
Founder **Fredrik Idestam**
Company **Nokia Corporation** HQ **Espoo, Finland**
www.nokia.com

The history of Nokia, one of the leading manufacturers of mobile phones and makers of mobile networks, goes back to 1865. That was the year that Fredrik Idestam built a wood pulp mill in Tampere, launching the paper industry in Finland. He built a second mill a few years later in Nokia, on the Nokianvirta river. Nokia Ab was established in 1871. The first logo most probably depicted a giant pike, which can be found in Nokia's waters.

Meanwhile, in 1898, the Finnish Rubber Works Ltd (*Suomen Gummitehdas Oy,* or SGTOY) was founded in Helsinki, but moved to Nokia in 1904 to start producing high-quality rubber galoshes. The two logos show the increasing importance of the company's place of manufacture.

Nokia tire production, ca 1970
Below left: Nokia E60, 2005

A third company, Finnish Cable Works Ltd, was founded in Helsinki in 1912. It initially produced imported copper wire, coated with a rubber-impregnated textile layer, and branched out into electronics in the 1960s. Jointly owned since 1922, the three companies officially merged in 1965, forming the Nokia Corporation. Nokia operated in five business sectors: rubber, cable, forestry, electronics and power generation. Its first logo was basically a simplified version of the SGTOY logo.

With the launch of the Nordic Mobile Telephone (NMT), the world's first international cellular network service, Nokia entered the digital age. The company presented a new corporate identity in 1987. Three 'arrows in flight' flanked a modernized logotype, which remains unchanged to this day.

In 1992, the company decided to focus on telecommunications and gradually divested the rubber, cable and consumer electronics divisions. In 1993, the slogan 'Connecting People' was attached to the logo. After a color change in 1994, the arrows disappeared in 1997, creating a stronger and cleaner look. A last restyling took place in 2005 when the logo returned to a darker blue and received a modernized font for the slogan.

1886 *(Nokia Ab)*

1904 *(Finnish Rubber Works)*

ca 1930 *(Finnish Rubber Works)*

1967

1987

1993

1994

1997

2005, Moving Brands

71 OPEL

1862, Rüsselsheim, Germany
Founder **Adam Opel** Company **Adam Opel AG**
HQ **Rüsselsheim, Germany**
www.opel.com

Founder Adam Opel started producing sewing machines in 1862. Proudly, he presented his initials on the cast-iron sides of all his models. He changed the logo several times over the following years, always keeping the entwined A and O. In 1866, Opel's product portfolio would be extended to include bicycles.

In 1890, the term *'Blitz'* (lightning bolt) appeared on bicycles for the first time. In combination with 'Victoria', the goddess of victory, 'Victoria Blitz' was depicted as the guardian angel of the cyclist on shields placed on the steering column of the bicycles.

In 1899, four years after Adam Opel died, his sons entered the new world of car production and introduced their Opel Motor Car 10/12 PS Tonneau in 1902, carrying the eye-shaped logo. In 1901, the Opel brothers also started to manufacture motorcycles, which carried the Opel script logo. This logo, slightly altered, would eventually also appear on the radiators of cars in 1909 - most famously on the 'Doctor's car'.

Two-cylinder motorcycle with 3.5 hp and electromagnetic ignition, 1905 (© GM Corp.)

'My Little Doll', ad for the 5/14 hp, 1914 (© GM Corp.)

Wilhelm von Opel wanted a strong logo that would symbolize both the company and the brand. This resulted in the laurel-wreathed 'Opel Eye' of 1910 realized by plant manager Riedel and Mr. Stief from the construction department. Apparently, the Grand Duke of Hesse gave Wilhelm the idea when he spontaneously started sketching during a chance encounter between the two men. The basic shape would remain unchanged until 1935.

The 1928 white and gold 'Opel Eye' enclosed in a red circle was developed for motor-cycles to set them apart from the more ex-pensive cars. From the mid-1930s on, a stylized zeppelin adorned the front grills of Opel cars.

1862

1890

1902

1909

1910, Grand Duke of Hesse, Riedel and Stief

1928

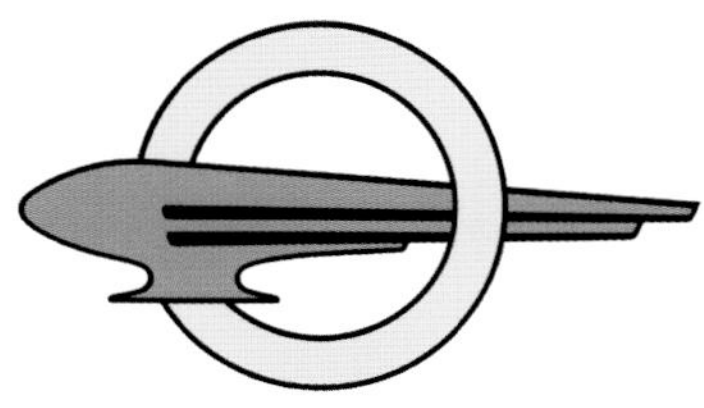

1937

1937

1950

1954

1963

1964

1970

1987 *(dealership and corporate logos)*

2002

2009, Mark Adams and GM Europe's inhouse design team

In those days, the zeppelin was the ultimate symbol of innovation. In 1937, the zeppelin was placed in a circle, symbolizing the wheel as a human mode of progression; this became the official Opel logo. Parallel to the zeppelin logo for the cars, a yellow-and-white oval-shaped logo was introduced on signs for Opel dealers. An evolved version also became the corporate Opel logo in 1950.

After 1950, the zeppelin became outdated and was transformed into a rocket-like shape, which became known as the 'Cigar'. Further abstracted, the 1963 logo hinted at a lightning bolt.

The following year Opel decided on a 'real' lightning bolt and restyled the logo, which evolved from the 'Blitz' brand name from Opel's light commercial vehicles, which were the first to carry the lightning bolt. In 1970, the Opel logotype and stronger Z-shaped lightning bolt were placed in a yellow square to form the next corporate and dealership logo.

The corporate identity had a thorough overhaul in 1987. The new lightning bolt, logotype and reduced use of the color yellow led to a stronger, ambitious and higher-quality dealership and corporate logo. The cars now carried the lightning badges on both front and back for greater brand awareness.

'Opel. Fresh thinking for better cars': this 2002 slogan marked a self-confident Opel with creativity, versatility, dynamism, quality and partnership as its core values and was visualized by a tapered 3D lightning bolt and subtle use of yellow for the brand name.

To update the brand's reputation and appearance, a new logo was introduced in 2009, together with the new slogan '*Wir leben Autos*'. While the shiny 3D badge with subtle branding kept the familiar Opel look, it is intended to better convey Opel's new focus on design and style. "Capturing that combination of beautifully sculpted shapes together with German precision is very much consistent with the overall design language and philosophy of our vehicles," explains Mark Adams, GM Europe's head of design.

Opel Flextreme GT/E concept car, 2010 (© GM Corp.)

72 PATHÉ

1896, Paris, France
Founders **Charles and Émile Pathé** Company **Pathé SA** HQ **Paris, France**
www.pathe.com

The symbol of the rooster was chosen by the firm in 1898. At that time, the firm was called Pathé Frères, the name of the first company founded by Charles and Émile Pathé in 1896.

The rooster symbolizes French national pride. In Latin, *gallus* means both a rooster and the Gauls themselves. The Gallic rooster is often considered the unofficial national symbol of France. The rooster was also a graphic illustration of Pathé's activity in the phonograph sector. At the time, cinema still constituted a secondary activity, so the sentence "I sing loud and clear" boldly appears above the rooster on the first phonographs.

The first rooster was designed by Louis Bienfait in the spring of 1898, but was first registered as a trademark in 1906 when the company was faced with increased competition and several cases of plagiarism.

As Pathé has been a multinational firm from the start, the rooster was often adapted to suit the company's various territories, activities and media. This situation consequently gave rise to a multitude of versions of the rooster, declining in number from the 1930s onwards.

In 1999, Pathé once again became a dynamic, innovative and living brand. Its identity comprised four main elements: the Pathé rooster, the talk and thought bubbles, a unique Pathé logotype and the exclamation mark. The bubbles are the visual expression of Pathé's voice and thought, asserting its independence. The logotype reinforces this spoken language. The exclamation mark recalls Pathé's innovative spirit, a constant source of surprises. When the Pathé rooster exclaims "Pathé!", it is a declaration of the exuberance and ingenuity of the Pathé spirit.

In 2010, the brand was streamlined and simplified by retaining only two logos (the Pathé logo and the P! logo) of the 10 that had been in use in 1999. The rooster is no longer depicted in realistic detail but is portrayed as a silhouette; it was baptised Charlie in memory of the firm's founder, Charles Pathé.

Generic Pathé poster, 1911
Next pages: Still from Pathé leader, ca 1999

1898, Louis Bienfait

1907

1924

1930, Ceccetto

1947

1960

1991

1999, Landor Associates

2010, Trinity Brand Group

73 PENGUIN

1935, London, UK
Founder **Sir Allen Lane** Company **Penguin Books** HQ **London, UK**
www.penguin.com

Penguin Books was founded by Allen Lane in 1935 as a publisher of affordable mass-market paperbacks. Initially an imprint of The Bodley Head, it became a separate company within a year.

The design of the books was essential to the success of Penguin, using a simple, recognizable grid of three horizontal bands for the cover. The top and bottom bands were color-coded (e.g. orange for general fiction, green for crime fiction, and dark blue for biographies), with a white band in the middle for the title and author.

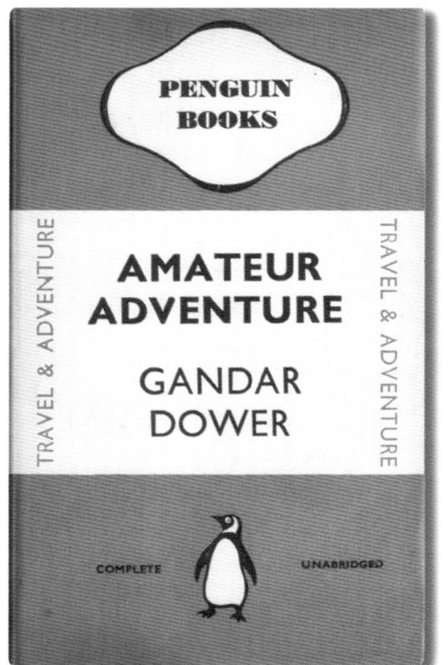

Early Penguin Books cover
('Penguin Books' set in Bodoni Ultra Bold), 1938
Top right: Cartouche with 'Penguin Books' set in Gill Sans

The top band held a cartouche with the company name, initially set in Bodoni Ultra Bold and later in Gill Sans, as were the title and author. The bottom band was the penguin's territory.

The initial design was created by 21-year-old office junior Edward Young, who also drew the first penguin based on sketches he made at the London Zoo. Allen Lane's secretary is said to have suggested using the penguin in the logo.

Over the years, many variations of the penguin were created and placed inside circles, ovals and rectangles: standing, walking, looking left and right, and atop an open book. There was even a curly calligraphic version.

Jan Tschichold, Head of Design from 1946 to 1949, played an important role in further developing the penguin, experimenting with a number of different versions, including the famed 1949 iteration.

The latest version of the penguin appeared in 2003, looking curious and standing flat on his feet. An orange background was added in 2010, when the company celebrated its 75th anniversary.

1935, Edward Young, 1935, 1937, 1938, 1938

1944, 1945, 1945, 1946, 1946

1947, 1947, 1947, 1948, 1948

1948, 1949, and 1949, Jan Tschichold

1950, 1967, and 2003, Angus Hyland, Pentagram

2010, Angus Hyland, Pentagram

74 PEPSI

1893, New Bern, NC, USA
Founder **Caleb Bradham** Company **PepsiCo** HQ **Purchase, NY, USA**
www.pepsi.com

Retro Pepsi sign, New York, USA, 2010

First introduced as 'Brad's drink', founder Caleb Bradham changed the name to Pepsi Cola in 1898. It is believed that the name was inspired by two ingredients used in the recipe: pepsin (a digestive enzyme) and kola nuts. Another theory is that Bradham bought the name for $100 from a competitor that had gone broke. Bradham's artist neighbour designed the first logo.

The big change in Pepsi's logo design began in 1940 when CEO Walter Mack came up with the idea of a new bottle design, with a crown carrying the Pepsi logo. In 1941, the bottle crown colors were changed to the national red, white and blue, in support of the war efforts.

The very popular bottle cap with the red and blue waves became the logo itself; the company would stick to that basic concept in the decades to follow.

The brand name was simplified to Pepsi in the 1960s. In the same period, the lettering was changed from a curly script to a bold, contemporary sans serif in an effort to move away from its main competitor, Coca-Cola.

The bottle cap was simplified in 1967 and then enclosed in a box in 1973, adding color with a red bar coming in from the left and a light blue bar coming in from the right.
It would get a small facelift in 1987, with an updated logotype and slightly bigger red and blue waves. All in all, this logo was the longest-lived Pepsi logo after WWII.

In 1991, the globe symbol was separated from the logotype and was made less prominent. The blue bar disappeared. The lengthened red bar and the globe now underlined the italicized Pepsi logotype. This strategic move in its battle with Coca-Cola aimed to appeal to younger generations.

1898

1905

1906

1930s

1941

1940s

1940s

1950

1962

ca 1967, Gould & Associates

1973

1987

1991

1996, Landor Associates

2003

2008, Arnell

In 1996, Pepsi launched 'Project Blue'. The background color on everything carrying the logo was changed to blue, beginning in several markets outside the US. In the centennial year 1998, it would be rolled out in Pepsi's home market. It seemed the most logical strategy for Pepsi to claim blue, as rival Coca-Cola already 'owned' red. The Pepsi logo was given depth by adding shades and shifting the logotype to overlap the globe.

Following the 3D route, Pepsi introduced a new logo in 2003 with a more dominant shiny globe and restyled, sharper-edged logotype with subtle serifs.

With the launch of the 2008 logo, Pepsi transformed the wave in the globe into what appears to be a smile. Pepsi also abandoned the 3D trend, as did Coca-Cola.

The globe has become the dominant factor, thanks to a slimmer, more subtle logotype. The classic wave can still be recognized as part of the letter 'e'. At first the globe took on a different smile on Pepsi's products: the basic logo for Regular, a small grin for Diet Pepsi and a big smile for Pepsi Max. Viewed as undermining the single-brand look, this difference reverted to one 'regular' smile for all products in 2011.

Tray with Pepsi drink cups, detail of 'Call your own time-out' ad, USA, 1970s

Pepsi-Cola
refreshes without filling
This holiday season, the traditional dishes will all be there—but how the recipes have changed!
The modern taste for lighter, less filling foods has affected even time-honored stuffings and desserts. And the slender waistlines of today's active people show how their wholesome eating habits have paid off.
Today's Pepsi-Cola, reduced in calories, keeps pace with this sensible trend in diet. That's why more people than ever this year will be asking for Pepsi—the modern, the light refreshment.
Never heavy, never too sweet, Pepsi-Cola refreshes without filling. Have a Pepsi.
Pepsi-Cola
The Light refreshment

Right: Pepsi cans with variable 'smiles', 2009
Below: Single Pepsi 'smile' for 2011 livery
Opposite: 'Pepsi-Cola refreshes without filling', ad, USA, 1956

75 PIRELLI

1872, Milan, Italy
Founder **Giovanni Battista Pirelli** Company **Pirelli & C. SpA** HQ **Milan, Italy**
www.pirelli.com

The Italian tire manufacturer Pirelli was established in 1872. Producing all kinds of rubber products, the company started making tires for bicycles in 1890 and expanded to cars and motorcycles shortly after.

A request from an American Pirelli representative to come up with a distinctive and memorable logo in an era of maximized advertising resulted in the idea of stretching out the initial P to form a roof over the other characters of the brand name in 1907. Pirelli also had a major success that year, with Prince Scipione Borghese winning the Peking-Paris car race on Pirelli tyres.

Without clear corporate guidelines on how to use the logo, it appeared in many variations according to whatever was popular at the time; the logos shown here represent only a small selection. The elongated P with its clever shift from thick to thin and back was a highly evocative way to portray the elasticity of Pirelli's premium products. Despite the variety, Pirelli had no difficulty becoming an iconic brand.

'Pirelli Stella Bianca', ad, 1930s

Although the number of variants diminished progressively after the 1930s, stricter rules were sorely needed. In 1945, following WWII, a strong, clear sans serif logo was created which has remained practically untouched until this day.

Pirelli is an official supplier of tires for Formula 1.
Shown here: the 2011 P Zero red supersoft compound, yellow soft compound, and grey hard compound

PIRELLI

ca 1906

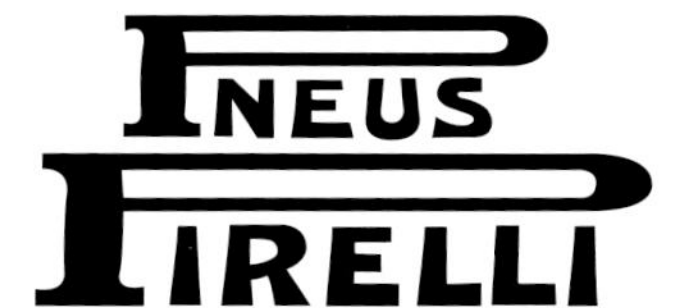

1914

1916

1917

1924

1920s

1930

1930s

1945

76 QANTAS

1920, Winton, Australia
Founders **W. Hudson Fysh, Paul McGinness, Fergus McMaster**
Company **Qantas Airways** HQ **Sydney, Australia**
www.qantas.com.au

Left: Fashionable stewardess, 1959 (Qantas Airways). Right: Qantas A380 over Sydney, 2010 (Qantas Airways)

The Queensland and Northern Territory Aerial Services Ltd was founded in 1920, initially operating air mail services in Queensland. Many variations on typographic 'logos' can be found from the early years, either with the full company name or the QANTAS abbreviation.

International expansion came with Qantas Empire Airways Limited (QEA), formed by Qantas and Britain's Imperial Airways in 1934. The logo showed a scripted logotype surrounding the Australian flag bearing 'QEA' and the Imperial Airways Speedbird icon.

The first kangaroo appeared in 1944 and was adapted from the Australian one-penny coin. The idea of the kangaroo followed the airline's decision to name its Indian Ocean passage the Kangaroo Service.

The 'Flying Kangaroo' of 1947, leaping the globe to symbolize the Australia-UK connection, appeared with the introduction of a new fleet of Lockheed Constellations. In that same year, QEA was nationalized. Accompanying the expansion on international routes in the 1950s, the need for a stronger brand led the airline to rebrand itself as Qantas and eliminate the globe from the logo.

In 1967, when Qantas Empire Airways changed its name to Qantas Airways, the logo was restyled, with the kangaroo enclosed in a circle or globe and a modernized logotype.

The wingless kangaroo of 1984 was placed in a triangle, following the shape of the tailwings of the Boeing 747s that made up the entire fleet by that time. The red triangle and bold logotype made a striking impression.

In 2007, Qantas unveiled its latest interpretation of its famous logo. The kangaroo was sleeker and more contoured, and its tail broke free of the triangle's edge. It seemed to be fitter and faster than the previous versions. The logotype was updated to match the style of the kangaroo.

NORTHERN TERRITORY AND QUEENSLAND

AERIAL SERVICES. LTD.

Q.A.N.T.A.S. LTD.

1920s *(both)*

Qantas

Empire Airways

1934

1944

1947, Gert Sellheim

ca 1953

1967

1984, Tony Lunn

2007, Hans Hulsbosch

77 RENAULT

1898, Boulogne-Billancourt, France
Founders **Louis Renault, Fernand Renault, Marcel Renault**
Company **Renault S.A.** HQ **Boulogne-Billancourt, France**
www.renault.com

Louis Renault and his brothers founded their car company in 1898. Launched in 1900, the first logo depicted a medallion with the interwoven initials of the three brothers: Louis, Fernand and Marcel Renault.

When the company started producing cars in large volumes, they incorporated a car into the logo. It was replaced in 1919 by the FT 17 tank, which Renault manufactured during World War I, representing power and victory.

The name was incorporated into the logo for the first time in 1923, in a grill-shaped circle, while 1925 saw the introduction of the diamond shape which forms the basis of the current logo.

Louis considered the Second World War and conflict with Germany as a mistake, so he capitulated to the demands of the German forces. As a result, Renault was nationalized in 1945, becoming the Régie Nationale des Usines Renault (RNUR). 'Regie Nationale' was added to the logo for the domestic market in both the 1946 and 1959 logos. It was removed from the logos altogether for exports. The company was privatized again almost 30 years later, in 1996.

In 1972, the Franco-Hungarian artist Victor Vaserely added a three-dimensional suggestion to the logo. His 'Op Art' logo, based on optical illusion, became world-famous.

In 1980, a corporate typeface was designed especially for Renault for use in all communications. In 1991, the 3D illusion suggested by the lines became a reality in a logo based on a 3D form, symbolizing innovation and quality.

The most recent versions of the diamond give a contemporary, photorealistic representation of the badge as it appears on the car.

Left: 'The best of both worlds.', ad, USA, 1960s
Above: 'Voila, Renault', ad, USA, 1982

1900

1906

1919

1923

1925

1946

1959

1972, Victor Vasarely

1980, Wolff Olins

1991, JPG Design

2004, Saguez & Partners

2007, Saguez & Partners

78 REUTERS

1851, London, UK
Founder **Paul Julius Reuter** Parent Company **Thomson Reuters** HQ **London, UK**
www.reuters.com

Removing the old logo from the Zürich office, 2008 *(© Reuters/Christian Hartmann)*

Paul Julius Reuter, a German-born immigrant, founded his news agency in London in 1851. He transmitted news and stock price information between London and Paris using a combination of technologies, including telegraph cables and a fleet of carrier pigeons.

The shield on the first logo was inspired by the coat of arms adopted by Reuter when he received a barony from the Duke of Saxe-Coburg-Gotha in 1871. In 1891, Queen Victoria granted Reuter and his heirs the privileges of the foreign nobility in England. The new Baron's coat of arms, granted by Duke Ernest XI, showed the globe, broken by rays of lightning coming from its four corners. Over a flagstaff gallops a horseman, spear in his hand. Underneath, a silver ribbon proclaimed Reuter's ubiquity: *Per Mare et Terram*. The accompanying scripted logotype was used until the early 1950s, interrupted only during WWII by an all-capital bold slab serif logotype.

Probably one of Reuters' best-known logos is the dotted logo of 1968, by Alan Fletcher. The idea came from the punched tape used in transmissions for conveying information at great speed. The punched system is based on a regular pattern.

In 1996, the dotted logotype was restyled and a roundel was added as a symbol to increase Reuters' visibility on computer and TV screens and to brand on-screen services. The roundel symbolized a globe, representing the worldwide nature of Reuters' business, and the continuous collection, processing and distribution of information, 24 hours a day. The dots represented the information and the two hemispheres day and night.

In 1999, the dotted logotype was abandoned in favour of a solid version. Appropiately called Julius, this font designed especially for Reuters improved on-screen representation. Bolder dots lived on in a restyled roundel.

After the merger with the Thomson Corporation, a new corporate identity was unveiled in 2008. The roundel now had a more dynamic feel by using gradually varying dot sizes forming a globe.

ca 1891

Reuters Limited

ca 1918

REUTERS

1939

Reuters LTD.

1946

REUTERS LTD.

ca 1953

1968, Alan Fletcher

1996

1999

2008, Interbrand

79 ROLEX

1905, London, UK
Founders **Hans Wilsdorf, Alfred Davis**
Company **Rolex SA** HQ **Geneva, Switzerland**
www.rolex.com

In 1905, German watchmaker Hans Wilsdorf and his brother-in-law Alfred Davis founded Wilsdorf & Davis in London. The forerunner of Rolex, this company manufactured pocket watches and 'travel clocks'. Wilsdorf came up with the name Rolex, a made-up name that was memorable, easy to spell and pronounce in any language. The first Rolex logo appeared in 1908, when the brand was trademarked. This typographic logo did not yet include the crown symbol. In 1915, the company was renamed Rolex as well. The Rolex company moved to Switzerland in 1919.

In the early 20th century, most wristwatches were merely a low-quality novelty item. Wilsdorf, an inveterate perfectionist, succeeded in producing personal timepieces of the highest quality, suitable for the most robust use.

The crown symbol (or 'Oyster') was registered in 1925 as an expression of prestige and unsurpassed quality, but did not appear on the watches themselves until 1939. It was named after the source of the crown jewel from beneath the waves, reflecting Wilsdorf's passion for the sea. Various Rolex watches still carry marine names, including the Sea Dweller, the Submariner and the Deepsea. Rolex is credited with creating the world's first waterproof watch in 1926, also known as the Oyster.

Both crown and Rolex logotype have changed a couple of times over the years, although they were only small steps to keep the logo up-to-date. The logotypes have always been designed with serif letters, from blocky fonts to the current slim, elegant incarnation. The same can be said of the crown.

Above: 'Eine Rolex Uhr zu Weihnachten'
('A Rolex watch for Christmas'), ad, Germany, 1946
Left: Rolex Explore II, 2011

ROLEX

1908

ca 1925

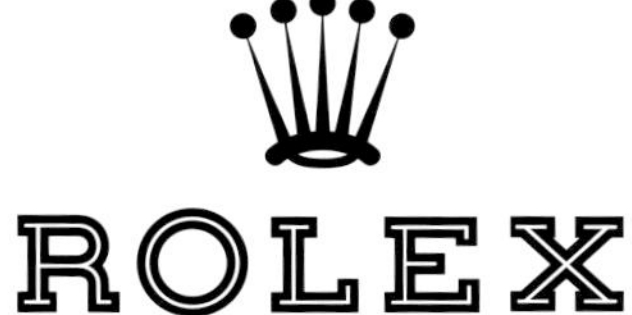

1946

ca 1950

ca 1952

1966

2003

80 SAMSONITE

1910, Denver, CO, USA
Founder **Jesse Shwayder** Company **Samsonite Corporation** HQ **Mansfield, MA, USA**
www.samsonite.com

Jesse Shwayder founded travel luggage manufacturer Samsonite in 1910, as the Shwayder Trunk Manufacturing Company, after working as a luggage salesman selling suitcases made by the Seward Trunk and Bag Company. Shwayder, a devoutly religious man, made folding card tables and furniture under the Samson brand, named after the biblical figure who was renowned for his strength.

The name Samsonite was first used in the late 1930s, as a product name for a line of suitcases called Samsonite Streamlite Luggage. Samsonite became the overall brand name from 1941; the company would later change its name to Samsonite in 1966. The Samson character was added to the logo in 1954 after initial typographic versions, together with the slogan 'strongest... lasts longest!'.

A new logotype that didn't include Samson was introduced in 1961, when the company expanded into the production and distribution of Lego building blocks for the US market until the arrangement ended in 1972.

The innovative character of the 1970s logotype proved to be the basis for next-generation logos. When the Shwayder family sold the company to Beatrice Foods in 1973, the logo was changed. A five-links globe symbol was added that is part of the logo to this day.

In 1996, the 'Worldproof' advertising campaign introduced a slightly changed logo in all dark blue with the addition of the new claim. Another advertising campaign, 'Life's a Journey', inspired the next logo update. The symbol was integrated into the modernized logotype and replaced the letter 'O', which resulted in a more compact and contemporary logo.

'Let the terminal be your runway', ad for the prestigious Samsonite Black Label, 2010

LET THE TERMINAL BE YOUR RUNWAY.
MAKE YOUR STATEMENT WITH Samsonite
BLACK LABEL

SAMSONITE

1930s

Samsonite

1941

ca 1954

Samsonite

ca 1961

1970

Samsonite

1973

1996

Samsonite®

2006

Samsonite was named after the biblical figure Samson, who was part of the logo from 1954 to 1960
Opposite above: 'Champions of carrying capacity', ad, USA, 1939
Opposite below: 'Round up a Samsonite set for mother...', ad, USA, 1954

Round up a Samsonite set for Mother...

MOTHER'S DAY IS MAY 9th

the Gift that carries your love

TRAIN CASE... for overnight ...for several nights...**$17.50***

Make it a *glamour gift* for mother this year—make her gift Samsonite luggage. So beautiful—it looks as if you spent the bankroll! Yet a complete set comes to about *half* of what you'd expect to pay for luggage of such fine quality. Or you can buy just one piece—and add other pieces for birthdays, Christmas.

All These Exclusive Samsonite Features: ★ "Better-than-leather" finish wipes clean with a damp cloth. ★ Packs more clothes in less space ★ Carries clothes wrinkle-free ★ Made to "take" rough handling ★

Also available in these finishes
- Bermuda Green
- Saddle Tan
- Alligator Finish
- Rawhide Finish
- Colorado Brown

A. B. C.

STRONGEST ...LASTS LONGEST!

ADMIRAL BLUE
A. Ladies' Wardrobe . $25.00
B. O'Nite (Regular) . . 19.50
C. O'Nite Convertible 22.50*

FLIGHT PROVEN PAN AMERICAN WORLD AIRWAYS

*ALL PRICES SUBJECT TO EXISTING TAXES PRICES HIGHER OUTSIDE CONTINENTAL U. S.

Samsonite *flight-proven luggage*

BY THE MAKERS OF SAMSONITE CARD TABLES AND CHAIRS

Shwayder Bros., Inc., Luggage Division, Denver 9, Colorado • Folding Furniture Division, Detroit 29, Michigan.

81 SHELL

1907, The Hague, Netherlands and London, United Kingdom
Founders **Royal Dutch Petroleum Company, "Shell" Transport & Trading Company Ltd**
Company **Royal Dutch Shell plc** HQ **The Hague, Netherlands and London, United Kingdom**
www.shell.com

Ferrari P4 in front of Shell signs at Le Mans, 1966

The Shell name first appeared in 1891 as the trademark for kerosene shipped to the far east by Marcus Samuel & Co., originally a company trading in antiques and seashells. When Samuel founded the "Shell" Transport & Trading Company in 1897, with quotations, he gave the Shell name corporate status.

The first Shell logo was a mussel shell. It was changed to a scallop or Pecten shell in 1904. Both of these initial logos were drawn realistically.

Both the word "Shell" and the Pecten symbol may have been suggested by a certain Mr. Graham, who imported Samuels' kerosene into India and later became a director at "Shell". His family adopted the 'St James's Shell' as their coat of arms after ancestors made the pilgrimage to the Spanish town Santiago de Compostela.

After the merger with the Royal Dutch Petroleum Company, becoming the Royal Dutch Shell Group in 1907, Shell was chosen to be the brand name with the Pecten as its symbol.

The shape of the Pecten has changed gradually over the years. Color was added in 1915, first appearing at California service stations. It may well have been Mr. Graham again who chose the colors; as a Scotsman, he would have been partial to the red and yellow of the Royal Standard of Scotland. Alternatively, the company may have opted for red and yellow as the Spanish colors, echoing the origins of many early Californian settlers, as well as the pilgrimage made by Graham's forefathers.

In the forties, the brand name started consistently showing up inside the Shell symbol, while the mid-fifties showed a start of significant simplification, which reached its peak in 1971.

The 1971 logo was designed by Raymond Loewy; his shell symbol is still in use today. The logotype changed in 1995, and the color scheme now used a brighter red and a warmer yellow, but the shape stayed the same. Even without the brand name, it is one of the best-recognized logos in the world.

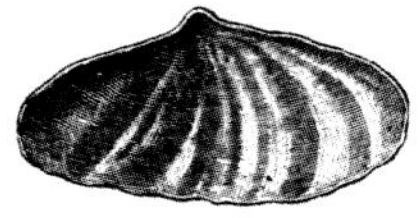

1900

1904

1909

1930

1948

1955

1961

1971, Raymond Loewy

1995

1999

Shell service station, UK, 2009 (Royal Dutch Shell plc)
Opposite: Shell X-100 motor oil, detail of ad, USA, 1952

SHELL
X-100
MOTOR OIL
PREMIUM-HEAVY DUTY
SHELL

82 SHISEIDO

1872, Japan
Founder **Arinobu Fukuhara** Company **Shiseido Company Ltd** HQ **Tokyo, Japan**
www.shiseido.co.jp

The oldest cosmetics company in the world was founded as the Shiseido Pharmacy in 1872. The word *'Shiseido'* can be translated as 'praise the virtues of the earth which nurtures new life and brings forth significant values'.

During the pharmacy years, until 1915, Shiseido's symbol was a brave hawk. When the company shifted its focus to cosmetics, the camellia flower was chosen because the company's best-selling product was Koyu Hanatsubaki hair oil; *hanatsubaki* is Japanese for camellia. The design was considered very modern, as most Japanese logos at the time were traditional patterns from ancient family crests.

The original camellia logo was designed by the company's first president, Shinzo Fukuhara, carrying nine leaves. Shiseido's design department staff simplified it several times until it was registered in 1919, and had seven leaves. Many tiny changes were made until the final version in 1974.

Many different logotypes were used in combination with the camellia symbol during the first half of the 20th century. In the limited selection shown here, it becomes apparent that the typical double 'S' with the elegant slant can be seen very early on. The current Shiseido logo dates from 1971, and it still feels very contemporary.

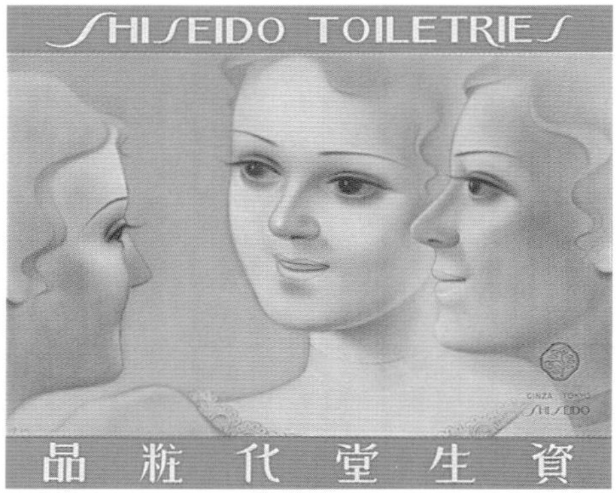

Above: 'Shiseido toiletries', ad, Japan, 1937
Right: 'Beauty Cake', ad, Japan, 1966
Opposite: The 1893 Kanji logo says "Kakkemaru", which means 'beriberi pill"; the logo is for a B1 vitamin deficiency treatment. "ANTIKAKKEUM" is a Japanese-English expression.
Next pages: Ad for water-based powder, Japan, 1920's

1893

1915, Shinzo Fukuhara *(final 1974 version shown large)*

1921, Toro Yabe

1924

1926, Shinzo Fukuhara

1927

1950, Mitsugu Maeda

1971, Ayao Yamana

進物用
化粧品

オーデネーヂ

衿、手、足などに
お使ひになつて
着物につかぬやう
工夫された水白粉

資生堂

東京 銀座

83 SPAR

1932, Zoetermeer, The Netherlands
Founder **Adriaan van Well** Company **Spar** HQ **Zevenbergen, The Netherlands**
www.spar-int.com

Dutch grocer Adriaan van Well started DE SPAR, as it was originally called, in response to the threat posed by fast-growing grocery chains. The idea was to unite the efforts of independent wholesalers and retailers.
DE SPAR stood for the company's philosophy: *'Door Eendrachtig Samenwerken Profiteren Allen Regelmatig'*, which translates into: 'We all benefit from joint cooperation'.

The Dutch word *'spar'* means 'fir tree', and it was this evergreen tree that was used to identify the organization from its very beginnings. The first logo includes a line in the red ring that translates as 'Shopping at The Spar means saving while you buy'. The text was dropped in later years.

In the late 1940s, the company's name was abbreviated to SPAR as part of the company's international expansion. The shorter name sounded stronger and had no pronounciation difficulties in other languages.

Spar store, China, 2011

Label for orange juice concentrate, Netherlands, 1930s

The 1950 logo showed a simplified fir tree and a more prominent SPAR logotype. The tree was later placed inside an unbroken circle, although it was oddly more complex than the previous version.

The final logo, which is used to this day, was designed in 1968 by Raymond Loewy.
In creating this strong, timeless piece of work, he streamlined the tree and let it flow together with the circle. He also eliminated any possible negative associations with prohibition signs by making it all green. By separating the symbol from the logotype, it was now possible to create a horizontal version of the logo, as shown on the photo of the Spar store.

1932

ca 1940

ca 1950

ca 1960

1968, Raymond Loewy

84 SPEEDO

1914, Sydney, Australia
Founder **Alexander MacRae** Parent Company **Pentland Group Plc** HQ **London, UK**
www.speedo.com

The history of the world's top-selling swimwear brand Speedo goes back to 1914. The Scot Alexander MacRae, who emigrated to Australia in 1910, set up an underwear manufacturing business and soon added swimwear.

During the 1920s, MacRae Knitting Mills introduced the 'Racerback' costume, allowing swimmers to swim faster. Staff member Captain Parsons came up with the slogan 'Speed on in your Speedos'. In that moment, the Speedo name was born; a year later, in 1929, the first Speedo swimsuits were being produced. The first logo showed a speeding curved and feathered arrow shooting right through the center of the Speedo lettering.

'Do what it takes to win', 2011 (explore.speedousa.com)

Thanks to early successes by the Australian team at the Olympics, the brand became very popular. In the following decades, the Speedo brand would increasingly dominate competitive swimming worldwide.

International expansion took off when Speedo Knitting Mills went public in 1951. The Speedo logotype was modified and an Australian touch was added by including a boomerang in the background.

The boomerang formed the basis of all future Speedo logos, looking faster with every restyling. Although there have been a few changes, the logo has remained remarkably consistent, proving the company made the right choice very early on.

1929

1940s

1951

1954

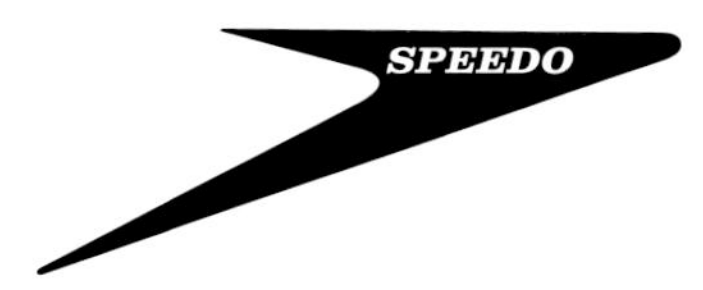

ca 1962

1970s

1980s

2004

85 STARBUCKS

1971, Seattle, WA, USA
Founders **Jerry Baldwin, Gordon Bowker, Zev Siegl**
Company **Starbucks Corporation** HQ **Seattle, WA, USA**
www.starbucks.com

The two-tailed mermaid or siren was based on a 16th century Norse woodcut, discovered by the founders in an old shipping book while searching for an interesting symbol for their new logo. It became the symbol for 'Starbucks Coffee, Tea and Spices', as the company was originally named. The name Starbucks was inspired by the harpooner Starbuck in Herman Melville's canonic novel *Moby-Dick*. The voluptuous, bare-breasted figure was associated with shipping (important for transporting the coffee) and was supposed to be as seductive as coffee.

With the merger of Il Giornale and Starbucks, the logo was up for a restyle in 1987. Terry Heckler was asked to do the design, both in 1986 and again in 1992. The circle, the stars in the ring and the dark green were taken from the Il Giornale logo, while the siren with the starred crown remained intact. Redrawn in a more contemporary style, the breasts were covered by flowing hair, taking no risks that certain people would take offense, but the belly button stayed.

The 1992 version had a closer view of the siren, focusing on her slightly uplifted, benignly smiling face. With the shift in focus, the tails' ends were simplified to more closely resemble fishtails.

A new logo was introduced in 2011 to celebrate the company's 40th anniversary. The outer ring with the words 'Starbucks Coffee' was removed, leaving the siren, now in green, to be the entire logo. Dropping 'coffee' was logical, since the company did a lot more than just serving coffee. Even so, removing the brand name was a bold move, putting the Starbucks logo in the premier league of brands that are so iconic that the brand name is implicit in the logo.

Left: Starbucks sign, Boston, USA, 2010.
Right: Starbucks' new livery, 2011 (Starbucks Corporation)

1971, Terry Heckler

1987, Terry Heckler

1992, Terry Heckler

2011, Lippincott and Starbucks Global Creative Team

86 TARGET

1902, Minneapolis, MN, USA
Founder **George Dayton** Company **Target Corporation** HQ **Minneapolis, MN, USA**
www.target.com

Initially founded as the Dayton Dry Goods Company, the Dayton Company opened its first Target discount store in 1962. Publicity director Stewart K. Widdess and his staff came up with the name a few months before the opening, immediately envisioning a classic bullseye logo.

Target's original bullseye logo consisted of three open red rings with a bold serif black lettering placed on top. To improve readability, the brand name was also placed beside the rings on store signs.

As Target expanded across the country, a streamlined look was introduced in 1968 with an all-caps Helvetica and a simplified bullseye with a red dot and one open ring, resulting in a more direct and memorable logo. By the turn of the century, Target had shifted its logo from two colors to a single red.

The pared-down bullseye proved to be such a strong symbol that the name Target became obsolete over time and may gradually disappear from the streets. The brand should not be confused with Australia's Target, which has the same symbol but different lettering in uppercase and lowercase.

Advertising campaign, New York, USA, ca 2008

1962

1968

ca 2000

2007

87 TEXACO

1901, Beaumont, TX, USA
Founders **Joseph S. Cullinan, Thomas J. Donoghue, Walter B. Sharp, Arnold Schlaet**
Parent Company **Chevron Corporation** HQ **San Ramon, CA, USA**
www.texaco.com

The Texas Company's first logo from 1903 depicted the five-point star, derived from the nickname for the company's home state Texas: 'The Lone Star State'. This state symbol was based on the 1836 flag of the Republic of Texas. In 1909, an employee named J. Romeo Miglietta added a green letter 'T' to the logo as a reference to the flag of Italy, his country of origin.

The 1913 logo incorporated the brand name for the first time. An explanatory variant served as a double-faced 42-inch sign at all company-owned filling stations. Gas stations were a fast-growing emerging market in an era of ever-increasing car sales. The next major change would not be made for another 50 years.

With the introduction of the first codified corporate identity in 1963, the logo had a dramatic makeover. The hexagon replaced the circle and the encircled T-star was reduced to a mere footnote in Texaco's history.

In 1981, with the introduction of the System 2000 stations, Anspach, Grossman and Portugal designed the new logo, again using the star symbol as the focal point. As an iconic brand recognized worldwide, Texaco removed its name from the logo in 2000.

Left: 'Tour with Texaco' brochure with 'banjo' sign, 1950s. Right: Texaco gas station with hexagonal logo sign, 1960s

1903

1909, J. Romeo Miglietta

1913

1913 *(logo for double-faced sign at filling stations)*

1948

1963

1981, Anspach, Grossman and Portugal

2000, Anspach, Grossman and Portugal

Visual from the 1953 ad
'For your fall change... see my dad!
He's a Texaco Dealer', USA

88 TOTAL

1924, Courbevoi, France
Founder **Ernest Mercier (Compagnie Française des Pétroles, CFP)**
Company **Total S.A.** HQ **Courbevoi, France**
www.total.com

In 1953, the Compagnie Française de Raffinage registered the new Total brand in Paris. The new 'Super Caburant Total' brand was launched on Bastille Day, July 14, 1954. The first logos emphasize its French nationality, with the colors red, white and blue.

A softened shape was introduced in 1963, known as the 'soap bar', with the lettering at a gentler angle.

To express greater stability and strength, the logo was restyled in 1970 with bolder lettering and horizontal design. The colored outline emphazised the 'soap bar' shape.

Broadening the patriotic symbolism, the color scheme was extended to include orange in 1982. The new logo with the diagonal bars symbolized "strength, assertiveness and friendliness", according to the company.

The renaming of the company from Total CFP to simply Total in 1991 brought a slightly restyled logo with a slimmer look and brighter color scheme. It was launched in 1992.

After mergers with PetroFina (1999) and Elf Aquitane (2000), TotalFinaElf was renamed Total again in 2003 after its strongest brand, an occasion that was celebrated with a new visual identity. The three interlaced 'streams of energy' forming and spanning the globe represented the three companies.

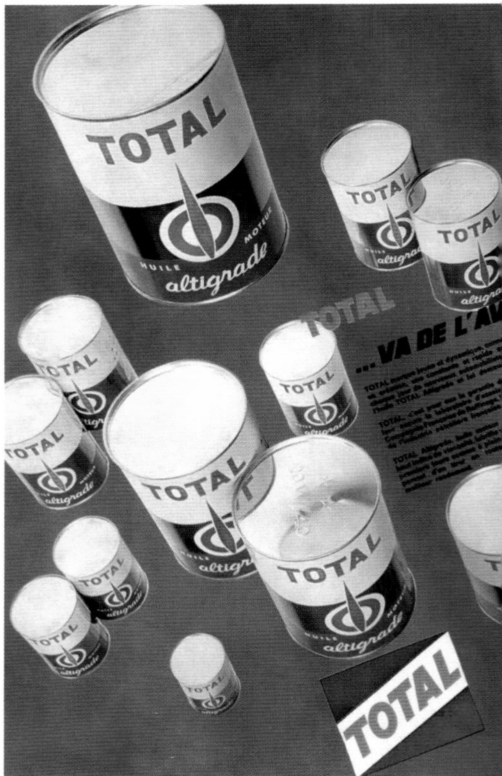

Top: 'Total...va de l'avant' *('Total goes forward'), ad for Altigrade oil, France, ca 1960*
Below: Truck at terminal, Nottingham, UK, 2006
(courtesy of Total UK Limited)

1954

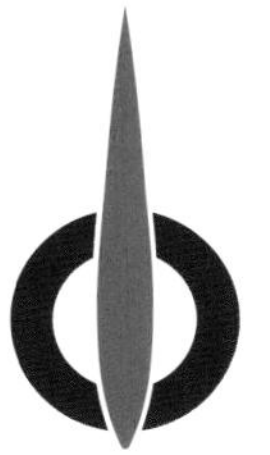

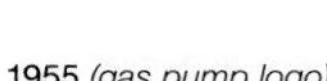

1955 *(gas pump logo)*

1963

1970

1982

1992

2003, A & co

89 TOYOTA

1937, Japan
Founder **Kiichiro Toyoda** Company **Toyota Motor Corporation** HQ **Aichi, Japan**
www.toyota.com

Above: Old TEQ logo on car rim
Right: 'When you first drive the Toyota Corona', ad, USA, 1970

The roots of the Toyota Motor Corporation can be traced back to 1926 when Sakichi Toyoda founded Toyoda Automatic Loom Works, Ltd. His son Kiichiro Toyoda started a car department and sold the first vehicles under the 'Toyoda' brand.

The 'TEQ' logo, with a font in the Katakana writing style, was chosen as the winner of a public competition for a new logo in 1936. Although pronounced as Toyota instead of Toyoda, it was thought to look cleaner, with only eight lucky strokes (Toyoda would have taken ten), and to sound clearer. The company therefore decided to take on the new name, also because 'Toyoda' literally means 'fertile rice paddies', so the slight change made it possible to avoid associations with farming.

Toyota entered the American market in 1957, but never used the TEQ logo internationally. Instead, a simple and clear sans serif logotype in Western writing was introduced. In some countries, Toyota used various combinations of both TEQ and Western-style logotypes, expanding this use to its home market of Japan from the 1970s on.

Lacking a distinctive and recognizable symbol, Toyota introduced a new logo in 1989, after five years of development. Besides forming a 'T', Toyota explained the ovals as "two perpendicular ovals inside a larger oval, which represent the heart of the customer and the company. They are overlapped to express a mutually beneficial relationship and trust between each other." The outer oval symbolizes the world embracing Toyota. Each oval is contoured in different stroke widths, similar to the brush calligraphy known in Japanese culture.

1930s

1936

TOYOTA

1957

1989

90 TOYS "R" US

1957, Rockville, MD, USA
Founder **Charles Lazarus** Company **Toys "R" Us, Inc.** HQ **Wayne, NJ, USA**
www.toysrus.com

In 1948, founder Charles Lazarus started a baby furniture store called Children's Bargain Town. He later introduced infant products and toys for older children. In the late fifties, he adopted the supermarket model for his store and changed the name to Children's Supermart.

Shifting primarily to toys, Charles Lazarus chose the name Toys "R" Us when he opened his second store.

The backward 'R', which much annoyed parents and teachers, was an attention-getter and was borrowed from the Children's Supermart logo. It imitates a small child's reverse writing of 'R', which is short for 'are'.

In 1980 a restyled logo was introduced without the exclamation mark and bolder, more condensed lettering. The color scheme also changed, although this is not the only color combination seen in this logo. Another version showed a blue 'T' and 'R'.

Like many other companies, Toys "R" Us was inspired by the coming of the new millenium and adopted 'Concept 2000'. While all older stores refurbished, a blue star was added to the logo, emphasizing the backward 'R'.

In 2006, the logo was altered again, now using more powerful typography and prominent 'R', with the star in it. The color scheme was also simplified, reducing it to four colors.

Toys "R" Us store with the giraffe mascot at the entrance, USA, 1990s

CHILDREN'S
DISCOUNT
SUPERMARTS

1965

TOYS "R" US !

1970

TOYS "R" US

1980

2000

2006

91 TUPPERWARE

1946, Orlando, FL, USA
Founder **Earl Tupper** Company **Tupperware Brands Corporation** HQ **Orlando, FL, USA**
www.tupperwarebrands.com

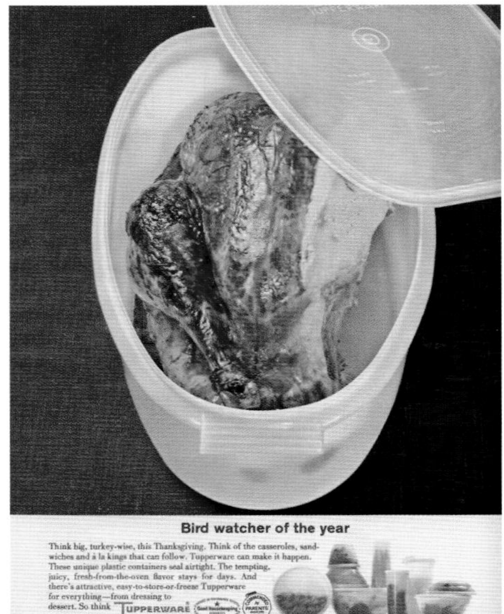

Bird watcher of the year
Think big, turkey-wise, this Thanksgiving. Think of the casseroles, sandwiches and à la kings that can follow. Tupperware can make it happen. These unique plastic containers seal airtight. The tempting, juicy, fresh-from-the-oven flavor stays for days. And there's attractive, easy-to-store-or-freeze Tupperware for everything—from dressing to dessert. So think TUPPERWARE
Think Tupperware Home Party. Call your distributor, listed under Housewares or Plastics, in the Yellow Pages, or write Dept. C-11, Tupperware, Orlando, Florida.

Inventor and chemist Earl Tupper founded Tupperware in 1946, manufacturing convenient, air-tight, sealed plastic food containers that were light, didn't break, and kept food fresh longer. The suburban 'baby boom' families welcomed the 'Tupperized', well-organized kitchen.

To boost sales, Tupperware Home Parties were held from 1948 on to demonstrate the miraculous products to consumers. By 1951, the retail channel was abandoned altogether.

Above: 'Bird watcher of the year', ad, USA, 1960s
Right: Tupperware Herb Chopper, 2011

The first logos were characterized by an all-capital logotype with an enlarged 'T'. The logo hardly changed at all until well into the 1970s, although minor modifications were made several times.

The logo was drastically modernized in the mid-seventies, when microwave ovens first began entering kitchens. The outlined logotype was now set in upper and lowercase, with each letter 'sealed' together.

In the new millennium, reaching nearly 100 markets worldwide and appreciating the increasing importance of internet, the company introduced a new logo. A typographic logo was used for the Tupperware brand.
An additional symbol, which resembles a dandelion clock, was used for the corporate logo, symbolizing community diversity, dynamism and the international character of the company.

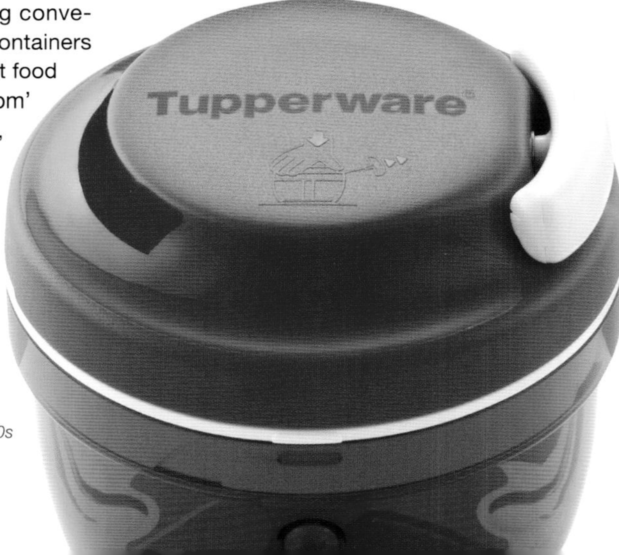

TUPPERWARE

1946

TUPPERWARE

1950s

ca 1958

ca 1974

Tupperware®

2000 *(brand and corporate logos)*

TUPPERWARE

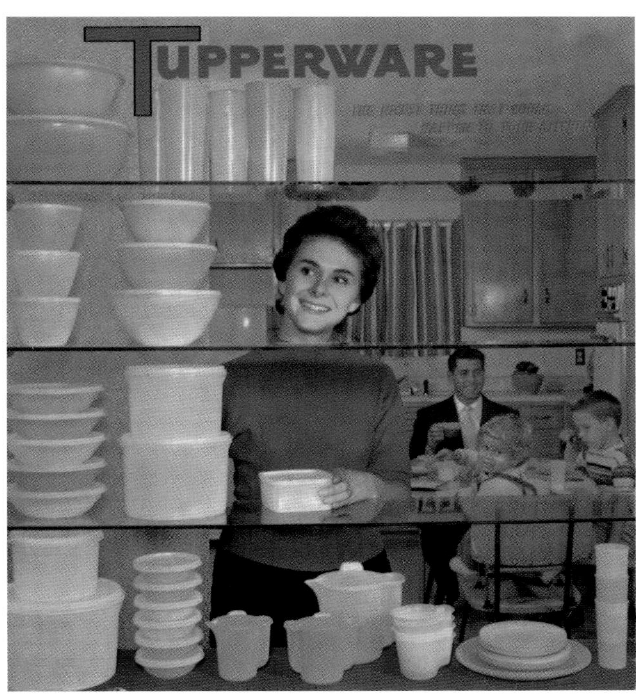

Opposite: Tupperware Home Party invitation card, 1940s
Left: Product catalog, 1950s
Below: Ad, 1950s

92 UPS

1907, Seattle, WA, USA
Founders **Jim Casey, Claude Ryan** Company **United Parcel Service Inc.**
HQ **Sandy Springs, GA, USA**
www.ups.com

Founded in 1907 as the American Messenger Company, the company changed its name to United Parcel Service in 1919. The first logo featured a shield and an eagle carrying a package with the promise 'Safe, Swift, Sure' on a side label. The vans were painted dark brown to make a stately impression, but it is said that yellow actually was the first choice. Since that meant the vans would always look dirty, the idea was abandoned.

In 1937, the logo was simplified to a shield containing the initials, with the message "the delivery system for stores of quality" to appeal to the retail trade. The addition of "since 1907" gave the security of a company with experience.

In 1961 Paul Rand shortened the shield, added a rectangular gift package with bow, and emphasized the lettering. The key to good design, he explained, was "taking the essence of something that is already there and enhancing its meaning by putting it into a form everyone can identify with."

In 2003, a 3D-style two-toned shield was introduced. The curve suggested the world-wide services of the company.

UPS package car, nicknamed by the comapny as 'The Big Brown Machine', Newport, USA, 2011

1919

1937

1961, Paul Rand

2003, Future Brand

93 VISA

1970, Delaware, USA
Founder **Dee Hock, Bank of America** Company **Visa Inc.** HQ **San Francisco, CA, USA**
www.visa.com

Left: 'Why is BankAmericard changing its name?', ad, USA, 1970
Right: Ad from the 'Go with Visa' campaign by TBWA, USA, 2009

In 1958, 65,000 residents of Fresno, California received a blue, white and gold striped BankAmericard, to launch the all-purpose credit card. The blue and gold were chosen to represent the blue sky and golden-colored hills of California, where the roots of Bank of America can be found.

By the 1970s, National BankAmericard Incorporated (NBI) had grown to become an international organization, though there was no unifying brand name. Each bank used its own name, using some form of the blue, white and gold flag. The Canadian banks, for example, created a pan-national brand. They issued BankAmericards under the name Chargex.

Dee Hock, BankAmericard's founder, recognized the power of one unifying global brand. He and his employees came up with the name 'Visa'. The three stripes stayed for reasons of continuity. In fact, the Visa logo hardly changed for the next thirty years. In 2000, the card-based logo was restyled slightly and a corporate logo with yellow swoosh was introduced.

As the bank card business was growing into a plastic-free industry, the literal picture of a card was too limited and a separate corporate logo proved confusing. A need for a brand framework that accomodated all payment types and services with one single logo for use in multiple environments resulted in a single new logo in 2006. The 'V' was given a distinctive accent by twisting the serif and the space-consuming borders disappeared, making the Visa name much more prominent.

1958

1968

1970

2000 *(brand and corporate logos)*

2006, Greg Silveria *(Visa inhouse design team)*

94 VODAFONE

1985, Newbury, UK
Founder **Racal Strategic Radio Ltd** Company **Vodafone Group plc** HQ **London, UK**
www.vodafone.com

In 1982, Racal Strategic Radio Ltd, a subsidiary of Racal Electronics plc, won one of two UK cellular telephone network licences, with the other going to British Telecom. The network was named Racal Vodafone.

The name Vodafone is a combination of the words 'voice', 'data' and 'phone', as the company delivers voice and data services for mobile phones. The Vodafone brand was introduced in January 1985, the first cellular network to launch in the UK. In the first logo, the white line bisecting the italicized all-caps logotype symbolized the network.

Racal Telecom, as the company was called in 1988, demerged from Racal Electronics as Vodafone Group in 1991.

In 1997, Vodafone introduced its so-called 'Speechmark' logo, designed with opening and closing quotation marks in the two O's of the Vodafone logotype, expressing communication.

After changing its name to Vodafone Airtouch plc, with the purchase of AirTouch Communications, Inc. in 1999, the company was renamed Vodafone Group again in 2000. A second logo appeared in 2002, showing a white logo inside a red rectangle with rounded corners and a cut on one side, referencing the shape of a SIM card. This logo was used for promotional material and store signing.

The logotype was redesigned in 2005, losing the quotation marks. The quotation mark symbol was restyled by reversing the colors and making the elements 3D, emphasizing the quotation mark by giving it shine and transparancy while keeping a matt solidity for the white circle.

Vodafone Group plc is now one of the world's largest and best-known mobile telecommunications companies. In line with that global recognition, the logotype is increasingly left out, leaving the symbol to stand on its own.

Vodafone store, Qatar, 2010

VODAFONE

1985

1997, Saatchi & Saatchi

2002

2005

2010

95 VOLKSWAGEN

1937, Kdf-Stadt (now called Wolfsburg), Germany
Founder **German Labour Front** Company **Volkswagen** HQ **Wolfsburg, Germany**
www.volkswagen.com

The origins of the company date back to the 1930s, when the German national socialist regime decided to motorize the nation by funding a state-sponsored 'people's car' (or *Volkswagen* in German) that anybody should be able to afford by taking part in a savings scheme. This ambition corresponded perfectly to a proposal by the famed car engineer Ferdinand Porsche.

Prototypes of the car, called the KdF-Wagen, appeared in 1936. KdF stands for *'Kraft durch Freude'* or 'strength through joy', and refers to a leisure organization of the German Labour Front (DAF), which was responsible for the car production. This car was the forerunner of one of the most succesful cars in history.

Volkswagen's first logo was designed by engineer Franz Xaver Reimspiess after an internal competition; he was paid 50 marks for his design. His V and W combination enclosed in a circle was submitted in a trademark application in 1938, and then developed to include a *'Strahlenkranz'* (radiant garland) and gear wheel for display at the 1939 Berlin Auto Show. The radiant garland and gear wheel were derived from DAF's *Kraft durch Freude* logo.

A new factory in the new town of KdF-Stadt (now Wolfsburg), purpose-built for the factory workers, had produced only a handful of cars by the time WWII started. During the war, production of KdF-Wagens ceased in favor of military vehicles like the *Kübelwagen,* which carried the gear wheel VW logo.

The *Strahlenkranz* logo was used as the corporate logo for the Volkswagen-Werk GmbH, while the simpler gear wheel logo was used as brand logo for the KdF-Wagen itself.

After the war, the car was officially renamed the *'Volkswagen'* and put back into production. Several VW logos appeared before the VW logo was finalized in 1948. A diapositive version was also introduced, with the VW roundel set in a square.

In 1978, the VW logo was restyled and an outline was added, which gave it more substance. The same logo could be used regardless of the background, unifying all brand messages. To modernize the brand, 3D versions of the logo were introduced. The final version to date was launched in 2007.

'Volkswagen, the quality car', brochure, Belgium, 1947

1938, Franz Xaver Reimspiess

1938

ca 1946

ca 1946

ca 1946

1948

1978

1980s

2007, Meta Design

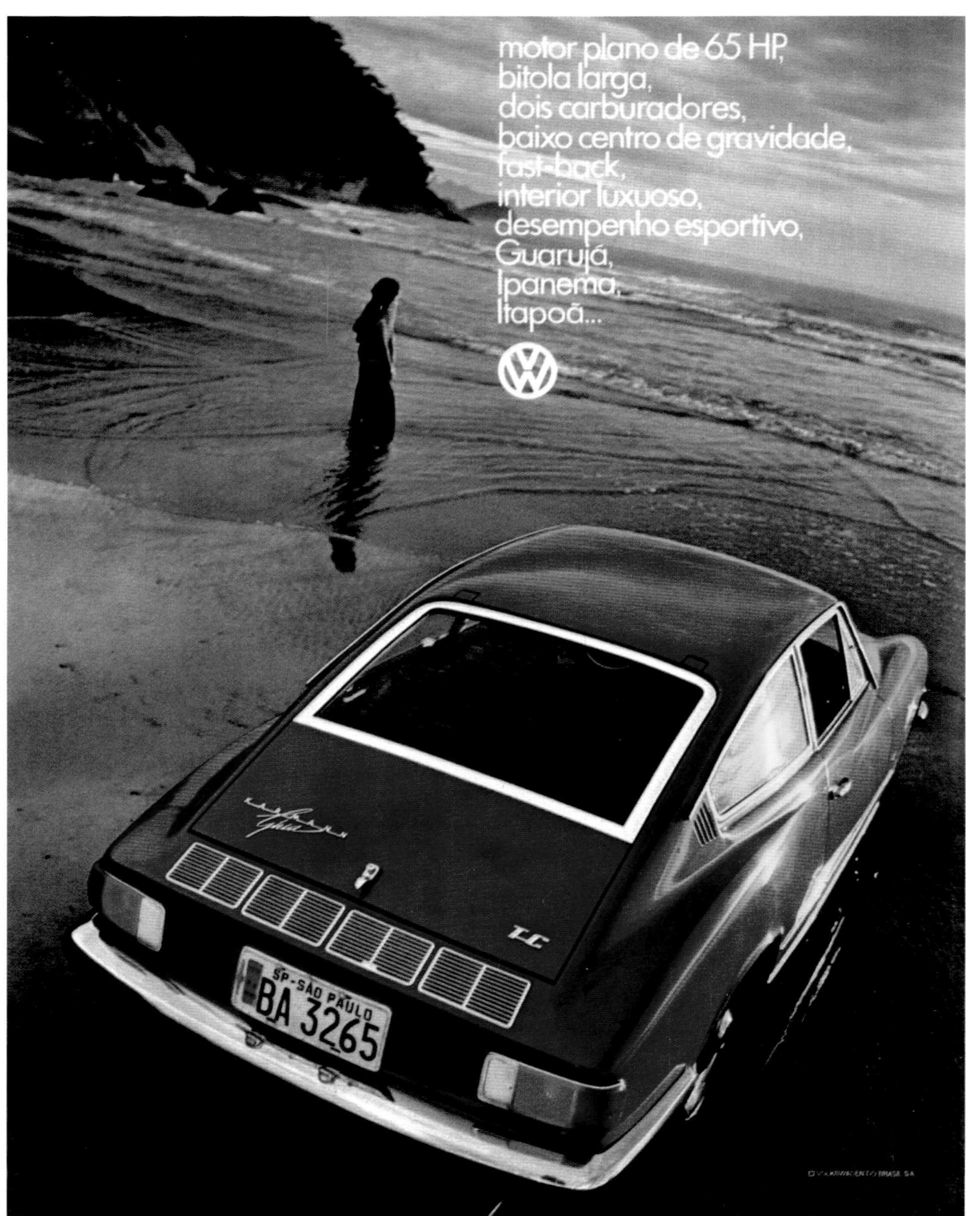
motor plano de 65 HP,
bitola larga,
dois carburadores,
baixo centro de gravidade,
fast-back,
interior luxuoso,
desempenho esportivo,
Guarujá,
Ipanema,
Itapoã...
SP-SÃO PAULO
BA 3265
TC

Volkswagen Karmann Ghia TC, ad, Brazil, 1972
Opposite: VW logo tech specs, 1948
(artwork recreated by Graham Smith, imjustcreative)

VW Trade Mark
Marque VW
VW-Markenzeichen
Signo VW
Simbolo VW
Marchio VW

110 010

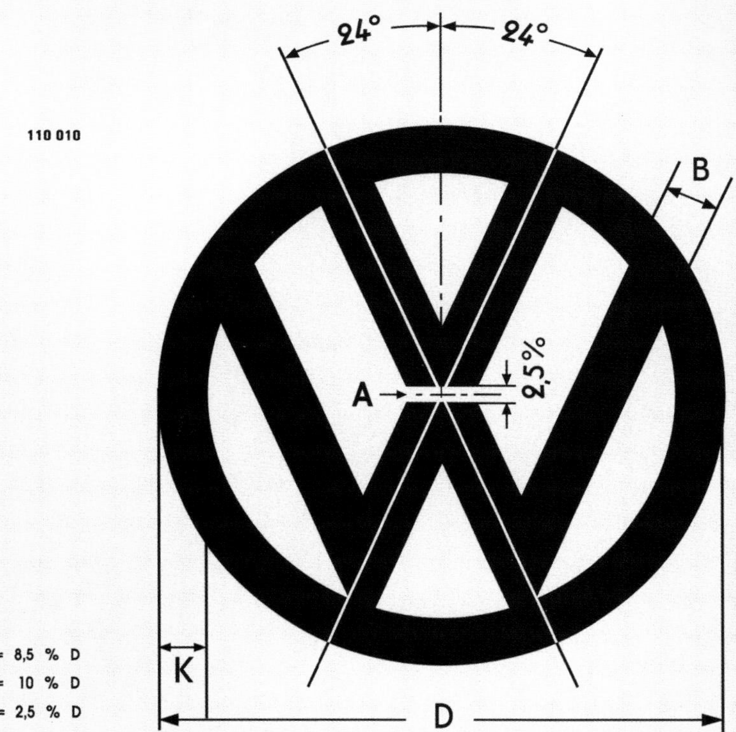

K = 8,5 % D
B = 10 % D
A = 2,5 % D

110 011

S = 150 % D
C = 25 % D

96 VOLVO

1927, Gothenburg, Sweden
Founders **Assar Gabrielsson, Gustaf Larson** Company **AB Volvo** HQ **Gothenburg, Sweden**
www.volvogroup.com

Sketch for Volvo PV36 brochure, 1934 (Volvo Car Corporation)

The latin verb *'volvere'*, 'to roll', becomes *'volvo'* or 'I roll' in its first person singular form. This ingenious name was simple to pronounce and would cause a minimum risk of spelling mistakes. The circle with an arrow pointing north-east is a pre-historic symbol for iron. It also represents Mars, the Roman god of war (weapons were mostly made of iron), and the male gender. Iron is an essential material in car manufacturing, since steel is an alloy that consists mostly of iron. The concept is easily associated with durability, quality and safety.

The first logo did not incorporate this symbol yet, but it was already used on the front grill at that point. The typical bold slab serif logotype was already part of the Volvo identity. The 1930 logo showed the 'iron' symbol integrated with the brand name, forming the basis for future logos. Remarkably, the logotype has changed very little over the last eighty-plus years.

The logotype even became so recognizable that the 'iron' symbol was dropped from the logo in 1970, only to reappear in 2006.

Volvo Concept Universe, 2011 (Volvo Car Corporation)

1927

1930

ca 1950, Karl-Erik Forsberg

1959

1970

2006

VOLVO

164

Top: Volvo PV444, poster, 1950s
Above: Volvo Air Motion concept car, 2011 (Volvo Car Corporation)
Opposite: Volvo 164, brochure, 1969

97 WALMART

1962, Rogers, AR, USA
Founder **Sam Walton** Company **Wal-Mart Stores Inc.** HQ **Bentonville, AR, USA**
www.walmart.com

The first consistently used logo for the discount store chain Walmart was the 1964 'Frontier Font' logo, with the characteristic Western style font in black, including an added hyphen. The Wal-Mart Discount City logo was used for print and apparel from 1968 until 1981.

Before 1964, the Walmart brand name was simply put in a variety of fonts, seemingly anything that was readily available.

The 1981 logo saw a change to a solid font, giving the company a more stable, established look. In 1992, the hyphen was replaced by a star in an all-blue logo. The star had associations with quality, ambition, activity - and of course the American national flag.

Aspiring to a more personal and inviting image, the 2008 re-design showed a very friendly-looking upper and lower case logotype set in one word. The bright blue type and warm yellow spark or sunburst icon added freshness and excitement. Expressing the new strategy effectively, the 2008 tagline read 'Save money. Live better.'

Top: Walmart store, 1979
Above: Walmart store, Moncton, USA, ca 2000
Below: Walmart store, Newport, USA, 2011

WALMART

1962

WAL-MART

1964

1968

WAL-MART

1981

WAL★MART®

1992, Don Watt

2008, Lippincott

98 WWF

1961, Morges, Switzerland
Founders **Max Nicholson, Julian Huxley, Peter Scott, Guy Mountfort, Godfrey A. Rockefeller, Prince Bernhard of the Netherlands**
Organization **World Wide Fund for Nature** HQ **Zurich, Switzerland**
www.wwf.org

WWF's Panda logo was designed in 1961 by its founder and chairman, the naturalist and painter Sir Peter Scott. The endangered species is a strong symbol for the focus of WWF's work: the conservation, preservation and restoration of natural environments around the world.

This first panda was the most realistic, with a shaggy fur and visible eyes. The name World Wildlife Fund, as the organization was called then, was not part of the logo, but spelled out as part of the copy. The logo was restyled several times in the 60s and 70s. Smooth lines replaced the furry look, while the eyes were simplified to black spots.

In 1986, the organization changed its name to World Wide Fund for Nature (except for the US and Canada), reflecting the broader scope of activities. As the initials were the same, WWF was now added to the revised panda. The outline was removed and the panda was adapted to look directly at the viewer, showing more emotion. This logo was more powerful and direct.

The restyling in 2000 showed an unchanged panda with the cuddlier bold sans serif logotype, better fitting the character and design of the panda.

To keep the brand alive and interesting for use in new media, the panda is now also used as a window, making it possible to work with different imagery and film to express the breadth of WWF's work and to show more of what goes on 'behind the panda'.

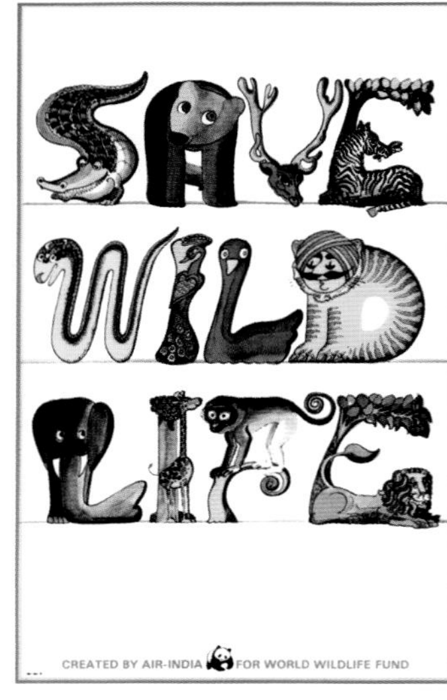

Left: WWF poster by BBH China, China, 2009. Right: 'Save wild life', poster by S.N. Surti, 1975

1961, Sir Peter Scott

1960s

1978, Lans Bouthillier

1986, Landor Associates

2000

2010, Asha

99 XEROX

1906, Rochester, NY, USA
Founder **M.H. Kuhn** Company **Xerox Corporation** HQ **Norwalk, CT, USA**
www.xerox.com

The forerunner of Xerox, the M.H. Kuhn Company, was founded in 1903 to make photographic paper; it was renamed the Haloid Company in 1906. In 1947, Haloid purchased a technology developed by Chester Carlsson to make copies on plain paper. Using a process known as xerography, the first photocopy machine went under the Xerox brand. After combining the Haloid and Xerox logos, the company name changed to Haloid Xerox in 1958 and to simply Xerox in 1961. The result was the block-capital logotype that formed the basis for future generations of Xerox logos until 2008.

The partly pixelated 'X', symbolizing the transition of documents between the digital and paper world, was introduced as a second logo to support the slogan 'The Document Company'. From 1994 on, the logo was red, which stood out better than the previous blue. The success of the digitized X logo and 'The Document Company' campaign started to become a problem, since people saw Xerox as solely a copier and printing company, while its focus had increasingly shifted to software and services. The digitized X and slogan were phased out of the logo in two steps. In 2001, the slogan was de-emphasized in favor of the logo, and was dropped altogether in the 2004 logo.

However, the logotype did not leverage in the three-dimensional and animated digital world of internet and mobile phones. A new logotype was created in the soft touch FS Albert font. A red globe was added with intersecting white and grey ribbons ('the connectors') encircling the globe, visualizing the worldwide connections between Xerox's customers, employees and other stakeholders. The objective was to make Xerox a more human and approachable brand.

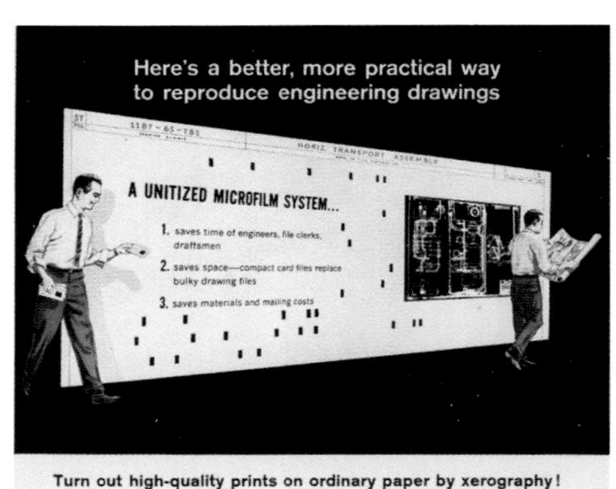

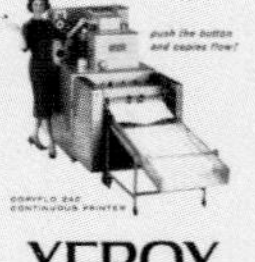

Above: Haloid annual report, 1949 (Xerox Corporation)
Right: 'A unitized microfilm system...', ad, USA, 1961

1926

1937

1949

1954

1958

1961, Lippincott & Margulies *(corporate and brand logos)*

1968, Chermayeff & Geismar

1994, Landor Associates

2001

2004

2008, Interbrand

ORIGINAL.

BELIEVE IT.

The one on the right is the copy.

It was made on the new Xerox 3600, a copier/duplicator that makes copies of offset quality at the rate of sixty per minute.

Every copy it makes is actually blacker, sharper and cleaner than the typewritten original.

It uses ordinary paper, like all Xerox machines, and it's as simple to operate as any of them. Even with accessories for automatic sorting, slitting and perforating.

We're now scheduling demonstrations to take place as soon as the machine is available.

The demonstrations are for everyone who'd like to see it take one minute to make sixty copies that don't look like the original.

XEROX CORPORATION, ROCHESTER, NEW YORK 14603. IN CANADA: XEROX OF CANADA LIMITED. OVERSEAS: SUBSIDIARIES THROUGHOUT LATIN AMERICA; IN ASSOCIATION

'Original. Copy. Do you believe it?', ad, USA, 1968

COPY.

BELIEVE IT.

The one on the right is the copy.

It was made on the new Xerox 3600, a copier/duplicator that makes copies of offset quality at the rate of sixty per minute.

Every copy it makes is actually blacker, sharper and cleaner than the typewritten original.

It uses ordinary paper, like all Xerox machines, and it's as simple to operate as any of them. Even with accessories for automatic sorting, slitting and perforating.

We're now scheduling demonstrations to take place as soon as the machine is available.

The demonstrations are for everyone who'd like to see it take one minute to make sixty copies that don't look like the original.

BELIEVE IT?

ATION, LTD., RANK XEROX LIMITED, LONDON, AND THROUGH RANK XEROX LIMITED, FUJI-XEROX CO., LTD. TOKYO. XEROX IS A REGISTERED TRADEMARK OF XEROX. 3600 IS A TRADEMARK OF XEROX CORPORATION.

XEROX

100 THE Y (YMCA of the USA)

1844, London, UK
Founder **Sir George Williams** Organization **World Alliance of YMCAs** HQ **Geneva, Switzerland**
www.ymca.net

The Young Men's Christian Association, as the federation of local and national organizations was initially called, was founded in 1844.
It provided low-cost housing for traveling Christian young men, and a safe place against the temptations of the big cities during the Industrial Revolution. It promoted evangelical Christianity and good citizenship by "building a healthy spirit, mind and body".

At the 1881 conference, the organization decided on the first logo. It featured the XP christogram and a reference to John 17:21, "That they may all be one... as We are one". The ring united the five continents of the world where the YMCA was represented.
Some ten years later, Luther Gulick came up with the equilateral triangle, which symbolized the unity of spirit, mind and body. It would be the basis for all future logos. The triangle would be integrated into the old World Alliance Insignia in 1895. The logo changed slightly in the following year and a second ring was added, which represented friendship and "love without end among individuals". In 1897, the logo was simplified to the famous logo with a white 'YMCA' in a bar crossing the red triangle. Although many typographic versions were used, it would stand the test of time for 70 years in the US, and is still used in some countries.

In 1967, a new logo was introduced for the YMCA in the US. The red triangle and a bent bar created a 'Y'. It is still the official YMCA logo for Canada, Australia, and New Zealand.

With the decision to change the name to simply 'the Y', as it was already nicknamed by the public, the logo received a complete make-over in 2010. The fresh and 'forward-looking' logo features multiple color options, expressing the great variety of programs the Y offers, for youth development, healthy living and social responsibility.

Soccer is part of many youth sports programs at the Y, 2011 (YMCA of the USA)

1881

1891, Luther H. Gulick

1895

1896

1897

1967

2010, Siegel & Gale

Many thanks to all those without whom Logo Life would never have been possible:

Angelique van Dam
Mats van der Vlugt
Marcel van der Vlugt
Kitty Vollebregt
Marcel van der Vlugt Sr.
Anneke van Dam
Niek van Dam
Edwin Visser
Rob Verhaart
Maaike Volders
Alco Velders
Joy Maul-Phillips
Martin van der Horst
Rudolf van Wezel
Lilian van Dongen-Torman
Heidi Boersma
Rens Kolkman
Dennis Neeven
Laura Willems
Joost van den Berg
Kitty de Jong
Anouk Siegelaar
Thomas Gruenewald
Wilfredo Bieren Jr.
Jack Jones
Laura Thorburn
Andreas Genz
John Entwistle
Katrin Hinz
Anne-Sophie Gerardin
Michelle Gauci
Gerline Diboma-Den Hartog
Tomi Kuuppelomäki
Susan Williams
Mutsumi Urano
Gerard Buschers
Yuko Nagase
Anja Schaller
Hugo Weenen
Uwe Schmidt
Achim Bellmann
Kathleen Hatfield
Erika Rosenberg
Lucia N. DeRespinis
Gerhard Vollberg

Ron behind the wheel of his dad's Mercedes 190, 1965

Ron van der Vlugt (1963) is co-founder and creative director of SOGOOD, an agency specializing in corporate and packaging design, located in the Netherlands.

He has 25 years of experience working on national and international clients such as Samsonite, Shell, Winston, Nike, Heineken, TomTom and Nissan.

Currently, he's working on branding and packaging projects for a number of brands from the AkzoNobel portfolio and Dr. Oetker.

If you wish to contribute information and materials for a possible (extended) future edition, please send an email to the author: *ron.vandervlugt@sogooddesign.nl*

You can also visit the Facebook page for Logo Life for more logo histories, articles, book reviews, and much more: *www.facebook.com/logolife.ronvandervlugt*

SOGOOD
Hendrik Figeeweg 1P
2031 BJ Haarlem
Netherlands
www.sogooddesign.nl

Logo Life at Piccadilly Circus, London, UK, 1962 (Andy Eick)...

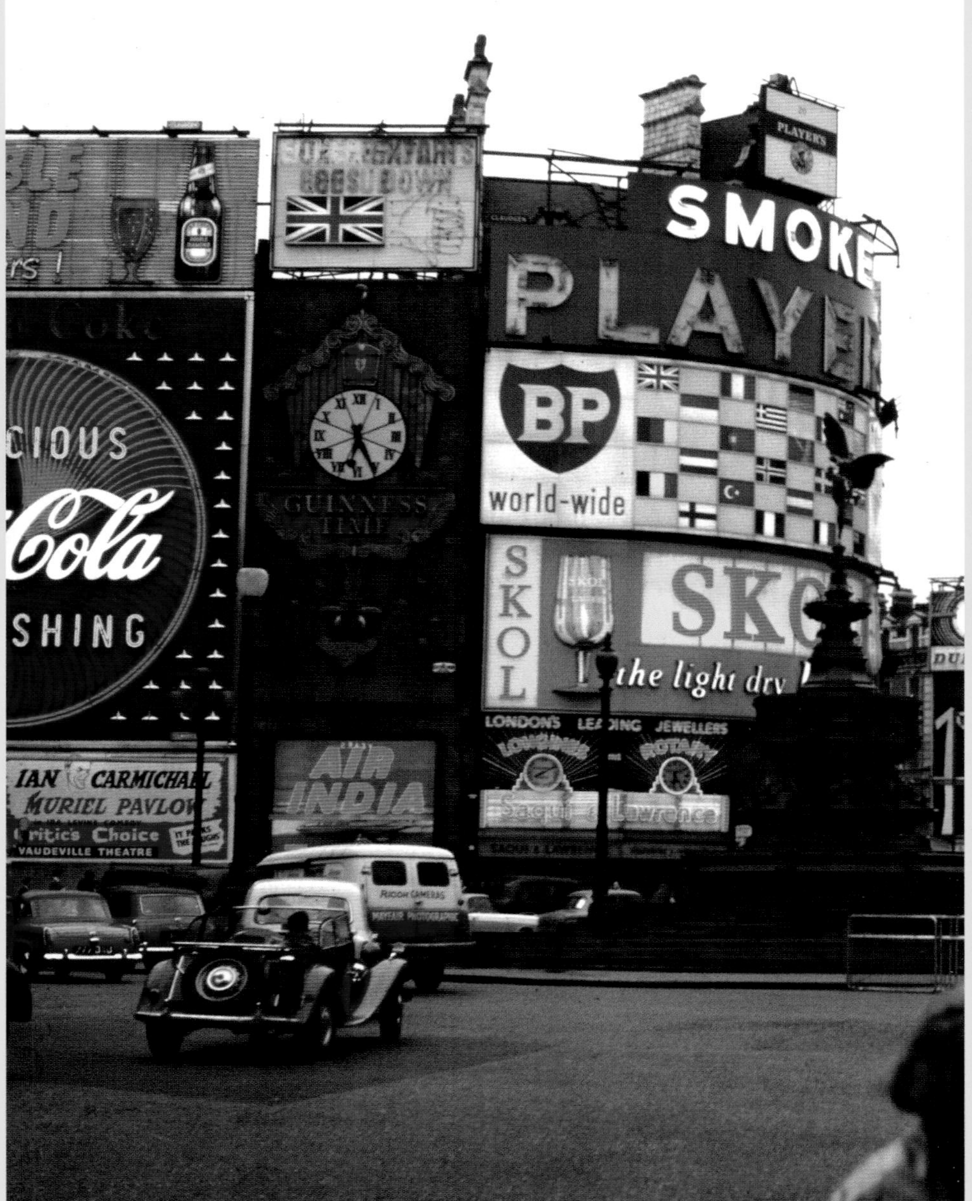

...and ca 2000

Enjoy
Coca-Cola
Coke
Enjoy more
Enjoy more
McDonald's
FOSTER
TDK
AUDIO & VIDEO TAPE
Carlsberg
Boots
LONDON PRIDE
London's Tourist Bus Service
HOP-ON HOP-OFF
AT 100 STOPS ON 7 ROUTES
ONE TICKET - ONE PRICE - VALID 24 HOURS
375
B115 ORU